Ontario Employment Law Handbook

An Employer's Guide

Tenth Edition

Ontario Employment Law Handbook

An Employer's Guide

Tenth Edition

STEWART D. SAXE, B.A., LL.B.

LISA STAM, B.A., LL.B.

LexisNexis®

Ontario Employment Law Handbook: An Employer's Guide
© LexisNexis Canada Inc. 2011
March 2011

Members of the LexisNexis Group worldwide

Canada	LexisNexis Canada Inc, 123 Commerce Valley Dr. E. Suite 700, MARKHAM, Ontario
Australia	Butterworths, a Division of Reed International Books Australia Pty Ltd, CHATSWOOD, New South Wales
Austria	ARD Betriebsdienst and Verlag Orac, VIENNA
Czech Republic	Orac, sro, PRAGUE
France	Éditions du Juris-Classeur SA, PARIS
Hong Kong	Butterworths Asia (Hong Kong), HONG KONG
Hungary	Hvg Orac, BUDAPEST
India	Butterworths India, NEW DELHI
Ireland	Butterworths (Ireland) Ltd, DUBLIN
Italy	Giuffré, MILAN
Malaysia	Malayan Law Journal Sdn Bhd, KUALA LUMPUR
New Zealand	Butterworths of New Zealand, WELLINGTON
Poland	Wydawnictwa Prawnicze PWN, WARSAW
Singapore	Butterworths Asia, SINGAPORE
South Africa	Butterworth Publishers (Pty) Ltd, DURBAN
Switzerland	Stämpfli Verlag AG, BERNE
United Kingdom	Butterworths Tolley, a Division of Reed Elsevier (UK), LONDON, WC2A
USA	LexisNexis, DAYTON, Ohio

Library and Archives Canada Cataloguing in Publication

Saxe, Stewart D.
   Ontario employment law handbook : an employer's guide
Stewart D. Saxe. — 10th ed.

Includes index.
ISBN 978-0-433-46557-7

1. Labor laws and legislation — Ontario. I. Title.

KEO629.S74 2006   344.71301   C2006-903580-6
KF3320.ZB3S74 2006

Printed and bound in Canada.

About the Authors

Stewart Saxe is a partner of Baker & McKenzie, a law firm with 70 offices in 38 jurisdictions, and member of the Labour, Employment and Regulatory Law department of its Toronto office. He is a well-known speaker and author on employment law topics. He is certified by the Law Society of Upper Canada as a Specialist in Labour Law and by the Human Resources Professionals Association of Ontario as a Human Resources Professional.

Lisa Stam is a lawyer in the Labour, Employment and Employee Benefits group at the Toronto office of Baker & McKenzie. She has spoken on a number of employment law topics and chaired several employment and pension law client and legal education seminars. She has extensive experience in the law on social media in the workplace. She blogs (www.canadaemploymenthumanrightslaw.com) and tweets (@lisastam) regularly on employment and human rights issues.

Acknowledgments

Credit for many changes to the various editions of this book, since its first publication, belongs to all members of the labour, employment and employee benefits group of the firm's Toronto office, including Kevin Coon and Cheryl Elliot.

In particular, we want to acknowledge the contribution of our colleague, Jonathan Cocker, as author of Chapter 9 on privacy laws.

Our thanks to the many members of the staff at Baker & McKenzie who have worked on the preparation of the text.

An Introduction and a Caution

INTRODUCTION

It is inevitable that as society becomes progressively more complicated, diversified and populated, laws govern a greater portion of our daily relationship with one another.

The 18th century common law governing the employer-employee relationship was relatively simple. The relationship consisted of the employer offering work at a particular rate of pay for the employee's labour and the employee providing the labour for the employer's wage. This simple contract could be terminated by either party at will, and its terms could be modified by express contract.

Early statutory restrictions on this contract arrangement were designed to protect the employer from employees demanding wages considered too high for the public good and to ensure that the employer had some notice of an employee's intent to quit. Legislative provisions for the benefit of employees did not begin to appear until early in the 20th century.

Our present law of employment reveals that we have come a long way legally, just as we have technologically, since the first days of the Industrial Revolution.

The law now provides minimum conditions of employment that affect virtually every aspect of the employment relationship. Legislation provides minimum requirements in areas such as worker health and safety and vacation entitlement. Another statute prohibits employers from discriminating on such grounds as age, sex and marital status. Furthermore, the law protects employees who combine into unions to bargain for rights beyond these legal minimums.

Additionally, both unionized and non-unioned employees are provided with statutory social security systems such as Worker's Compensation, Employment Insurance and the Canada Pension Plan.

The employer who just wants to get on with making picture frames, or running a hotel, is likely to find these laws to be a confusing labyrinth. The confusion is not helped by the fact that some of these provisions run contrary to what he or she was taught on father's or mother's knee.

It is for the employer who is wondering how to fire the sales manager, or whether it is compulsory to give employees two weeks' paid vacation, or what can be done about a notice that a union has applied to represent employees, that this book is written.

THE CAUTION

The law discussed in this book is constantly changing. These changes are the result of statutory and regulatory changes, or the result of new decisions by the courts and tribunals responsible for applying the law to every day situations.

Some parts of this book may therefore become outdated with time. For this reason, as well as the complicated nature of real-life situations, it must never be assumed that any text, including this one, provides a complete answer to any particular problem.

The law in this edition is as at January 1, 2011.

Table of Contents

Chapter 2
FURTHER MINIMUM TERMS OF EMPLOYMENT

Chapter 5
EMPLOYMENT CONTRACTS AND TERMINATION OF
NON-UNION EMPLOYEES

Chapter 6
THE ARRIVAL OF A TRADE UNION

Chapter 9
PRIVACY LAW

Chapter 1

The Employment Standards Act, 2000

DOES THE ACT APPLY?

The Ontario *Employment Standards Act* sets out minimum terms and conditions of employment that apply to most employees in the province. It is very important to note that the Act provides only minimums, and better terms may exist under a contract of employment (either actual or presumed to exist by the common law); employer practices or collective agreements.

The Act does not apply to:

(a) employees covered by federal employment law. This includes employees of the federal government and federal Crown corporations, employees engaged in the telecommunications industry (*e.g.*, telephone, radio, television), employees engaged in international or inter-provincial transportation (*e.g.*, airlines, railways, bus and trucking companies operating across borders), and bank employees. The *Canada Labour Code* applies to such employees, and for the most part its provisions are similar to the Ontario Act;

(b) diplomats; holders of political, religious or judicial office; or elected officials of an organization (including a trade union);

(c) high school, college and university students on work experience programs;

(d) inmates on work projects or participants in rehabilitation programs; and

(e) police officers (except for the section regarding lie detector tests which has certain requirements).

Only certain specified sections apply to provincial government employees, including the Leaves of Absences and Employment Termination provisions.

The Act only applies to employment relationships, not to the hiring of independent contractors. The distinction is not always easy to make. Various legal tests are used to distinguish independent contractors from true employees. One common test is whether the individual has a chance of profiting from his or her venture and, conversely, risking a loss. This same test also looks at whether the individual supplies his or her own tools of the trade. Finally, this test considers the extent of control exercised by the "employer" over the individual. Is the individual free to elect his or her own way of doing the job? If the individual has no chance of profit, or risk of loss; if he or she uses equipment supplied by the "employer", and if the "employer" can control how the job is done, then the individual is almost certainly an "employee".

Another more recent approach is to ask whether the work performed by the person is an integral part of the organization. If it is, the person is probably an employee. When, as is often the case, the answers are not clear, the determination of employment status can be difficult.

Generally, employees cannot agree to give up their rights under the Act. However, where the terms or conditions of employment found either in a collective agreement or in a contract of employment (whether oral or written) provide a greater right or benefit than required by the Act in regard to a particular right, then the contract or collective agreement prevails. This may mean that a specific benefit under the Act is not available to a particular employee. If, for example, an employee is covered by a collective agreement that provides for 11 paid holidays (the Act provides for nine) but does not include Victoria Day as one of them (as the Act does) the employee would be precluded from claiming Victoria Day because the agreement provided a greater benefit. However, rights cannot be traded between each other, so an employer providing greater vacation rights cannot provide fewer holidays.

Specific exemptions from the Act's provisions also exist in some cases in regard to particular rights. The most common of these are dealt with in the sections following that deal with those rights.

PAYMENT OF WAGES

The Act requires employers to establish a regular pay period and pay day and to pay earned wages, not including vacation pay, at such time. Payment may be made by cash, cheque or by direct deposit to an account in the employee's name at a nearby financial institution (unless the employee agrees to one not nearby).

With each wage payment the employee is entitled to a statement setting out the details of the wage calculation.

Upon termination of employment the employee is entitled to all wages, including vacation pay, owing by the next pay day, or within seven days if that is longer. Payment of severance pay can be made over a period of up to three years with the agreement of the employee or the approval of the Director of Employment Standards. This is dealt with in the severance pay section below.

DEDUCTIONS FROM WAGES

The Act limits the right of an employer to make wage deductions from an employee's pay. Deductions are allowed if they are:

- pursuant to a court order (for example, garnishee order);
- required by statute law (for example, *Income Tax Act, Canada Pension Plan, Employment Insurance Act*); or
- with the employee's written authorization.

Employee authorizations must specify the sum to be deducted or set out a formula that allows the sum to be calculated.

Employee authorizations to deduct are not allowed for faulty work or for lost property or cash shortages where someone other than the employee had access to the cash or property. This last limitation has been very strictly applied in some decided cases.

RECORDS

The Act requires that most records be kept for three years after the employee ceases to be employed by the employer or the date to which the information relates. However, employers must consider the application of other laws before disposing of records, including the *Income Tax Act*, the *Occupational Health and Safety Act* and the possibility of being sued in court. As a result, unless record retention is a burden, most records should be kept for at least seven years. In burdensome situations the application of the law to each type of record must be carefully reviewed. Occupational Health records must be retained for 50 years.

The Act requires that the employer establish and maintain a record, and keep it for three years following termination, which includes the employee's name, address and start date. In addition, a record of wage calculation information and the employee's hours of work (unless salaried) records must be kept for three years following the pay period. Vacation time and pay records must also be kept for three years, as must all records regarding leaves of absence.

The records must be available for inspection by an officer of the Employment Standards Branch in Ontario. The Branch has accepted situations where the record can be viewed on a terminal and printed out in Ontario.

Employers who fail to make and retain the records required are, among other things, subject to set fines that range up to $1,000 per employee for repeat offenders.

HOURS OF WORK

Exemptions

The Act sets limits as to how many hours an employee can work each day and each week. These limits are not to be confused with the requirement to pay overtime premiums; that requirement is dealt with separately below.

Certain employees are exempt from the hours of work provisions. They include:[1]

List One:

- qualified professionals in: architecture, law, professional engineering, public accounting, surveying, veterinary science, chiropody, chiropractic, dentistry, massage therapy, medicine, optometry, pharmacy, physiotherapy and psychology;
- teachers;
- students in training for any of the above;
- employees engaged in commercial fishing;
- registered real estate brokers;
- commission salespersons making offers to purchase or sell goods or services away from the company's place of business, except route salespersons;
- information technology professionals;[2]
- employees in the recorded visual and audio-visual entertainment production industry; or
- most farm workers, horse breeders and flower growers.

Also exempt[3] from the hours of work requirements, except the entitlement to an eating period, are the following employees:

List Two:

- managers and supervisors;
- construction employees;
- firefighters;
- fishing and hunting guides;
- resident superintendents and caretakers of residential buildings; and
- funeral directors and employees.

---

[1]   This first list of exemptions is referred to as "list one" in later sections.

[2]   An information technology professional includes employees engaged in the design, management or operation of information systems based on computers or related technologies who use specialized knowledge and professional judgment.

[3]   This second list is referred to as "list two" in later sections.

Landscape gardeners and those installing or maintaining swimming pools are exempt, except for the eating period entitlement and the entitlement to at least 11 hours off work each day.

There are special rules for homemakers (persons employed to perform homemaking services in a private residence) and residential care workers.

The exemption of managers and supervisors is the most common of the exemptions. It applies to persons whose work is managerial or supervisory even though they may perform non-managerial or non-supervisory tasks on an irregular or exceptional basis. This creates a separation line similar to, but not the same as, the U.S. distinction between "exempt" and "non-exempt" employees. Significant litigation over this exemption is expected in coming years.

The concept of "managerial" work is generally accepted to include very senior staff who may not actually manage anyone. Thus, a Director of Human Resources or of Policy and Planning who has no one who directly reports to them, will still be exempt.

The Requirements

The number of hours an employee can be required to work is limited to the company's established regular workday or to eight hours, where no regular workday is established. It is also limited to a maximum of 48 hours per week. A regular workday may be established that is up to 13 hours long.

With the employee's written agreement and the approval of the Director of Employment Standards the limits can be exceeded so long as no more than 60 hours are worked per week. Such special agreements can be revoked by the employee with two weeks written notice. Special agreements to exceed the 60-hour limit are possible with the approval of the Director. In obtaining employee approval, the employee must be given a government information brochure about their rights and acknowledge that they are aware of those rights.

Employees must have 11 hours off work each day and at least eight hours off between shifts unless the total time worked on successive shifts is 13 hours or less, or unless the employee agrees otherwise in writing.

Employees must also have either 24 consecutive hours off each week or 48 consecutive hours off every two consecutive weeks.

The above rules do not apply:

- in emergencies;
- in unforeseen circumstances, to ensure essential public services;
- in unforeseen circumstances, to maintain continuous processes or seasonal operations; and
- if the employee is needed to carry out urgent repair work to plant or equipment.

Employees are entitled to a 30-minute unpaid eating period every five hours. With the employee's permission (which need not be written) this can be split into two periods. There is no entitlement in the Act to other breaks, such as "smoking" or "rest" breaks.

OVERTIME PAY

All the exemptions set out as "list one" and "list two" in the above "Hours of Work" sections, as well as the exemption of landscape gardeners, also apply to the overtime pay requirements.

While the hours of work provisions do not apply to construction employees, the overtime pay rules do apply in the construction industry.

Taxi cab drivers, ambulance crew and students employed to supervise children have a special exemption from the overtime provisions.

The general rule is that overtime pay at the rate of at least time and one-half must be paid for all hours worked in excess of 44 hours per week.

With the employee's agreement in writing, the number of hours worked per week may be averaged over separate, non-overlapping periods of two or more consecutive weeks. There is no maximum but four is the practical threshold. This ability to average hours worked is critical to most 12-hour shift systems. Note, however, that averaging systems require the approval of the Director of Employment Standards for the program.

The employees' averaging agreement may be contained in a collective agreement. For non-union employees written agreements are required with specific expiry dates not more than two years later. Such agreements are renewable.

It is important for these, and all required employee agreements, that the employee understands the agreement and its impact. The employer must be able to prove, in the circumstances, that agreements were understood when signed.

Rather than overtime payments, the employer and the employee can agree in writing to one and one-half times the overtime hours worked as paid time off. Such time off will have to be scheduled within three months unless agreed to be within 12 months. If employment ends before the time off is scheduled, then the overtime payment will have to be made.

There are special overtime rules for certain types of employment, including:

- road building construction;
- sewer and water main construction;
- employees in hotels, motels, resorts, restaurants or taverns provided with room and board who work 24 weeks or less per year;
- seasonal employees doing fruit and vegetable processing;
- workers employed by companies in the business of local cartage or highway transport; and

• homemakers (persons employed to perform household services in a private residence) and residential care workers.

MINIMUM WAGE

The Act requires that employers pay at least the minimum wage to all employees. Special exemptions apply to:

• students employed in a recreational program operated by a charity;
• students employed to supervise children or students employed at a children's camp; and
• caretakers of residential buildings living in the building.

The categories in list one (see "Hours of Work" above) are also exempt.

There are a number of different minimum wages. Unless a specific minimum wage exists, the general minimum applies. Specific minimums are provided for:

• employees serving liquor;
• hunting or fishing guides;
• homeworkers; and
• students under 18 years of age during their school holiday or employed for less than 28 hours per week.

The actual minimums are increased regularly. For the current levels, call the Employment Standards Branch. In Toronto, this number is (416) 326-7160; outside Toronto check the telephone book listing under "Government of Ontario, Ministry of Labour".

As of March 31, 2010, the general minimum is $10.25 per hour.

Where room and board are provided, these may be valued by the employer in determining whether the minimum wage is being paid. Currently in 2010, the allowable values in most circumstances are:

Room — $31.70 per week
Shared room — $15.85 per week
Meals — $2.55 each to a maximum of $53.55 per week
Both a room and meals — $85.25 per week for a private room and $69.40 per week for a shared room.

A special room and board rule applies to fruit, vegetable and tobacco harvesters.

PUBLIC HOLIDAYS

"Public holidays" and "vacations" are two different concepts under the Act. Public holidays are specific days of the year that the Act defines as a public holiday for most employees in Ontario. Vacation days, however, are those days taken by an individual employee and are discussed in the section below.

The exemptions in "list one" under "Hours of Work" above, apply to the entitlement to public holidays, except that teachers, who, while exempt from the Act, will be entitled to certain public holidays under the *Education Act*. The exemptions in "list two" also apply, except that managers, supervisors, funeral directors and employees, and information technology professionals are not exempt and are therefore entitled to public holiday pay.

Taxi cab drivers are exempt, ambulance crew are not (the holidays requirement applies to them). Landscape gardeners and those installing or maintaining swimming pools, as well as students supervising children are exempt.

Construction industry employees are exempt if paid 7.7 per cent of their wages as a vacation pay/public holiday pay replacement.

There are special rules for employees in the women's coat and suit industry, in the women's dress and sportswear industry, for those employees paid on a piece-work basis and for homeworkers. These employees are all paid "industry holiday" pay rather than public holiday pay.

Seasonal employees of a hotel, motel, resort, restaurant or tavern provided with room and board are exempt from the entitlement to public holiday pay.

The former exemption for persons employed under an arrangement whereby they may or may not "elect to work" — when requested (such as most on-call banquet employees in the hospitality industry) was revoked in January 2009. Thus, "elect to work" employees, as well as "on-call" employees who do work on a public holiday are entitled to public holiday pay.

Finally, in November 2009, a new section was added to the Act that addresses temporary help agencies and their employees. Prior to the new section, most temporary agency employees fell under the "elect to work" provisions referred to in the previous paragraph, and thus, have been entitled to holiday pay since the "elect to work" exemption was revoked in January 2009.

The new section in the Act clarifies the following additional requirements regarding temporary employees employed by a temporary help agency (called an "assignment employee"):

- during an assignment by the temporary help agency to a company (*i.e.*, to a client of the temporary help agency), the temporary help agency remains the "employer" to the assignment employee and is therefore responsible for wages, including holiday pay entitlements;
- an assignment employee will be entitled to public holiday pay if he or she is on assignment by the temporary help agency to a company (*i.e.*, a client

of the temporary help agency), provided the usual criteria described below are met, such as working the regularly assigned day before or after the public holiday;

- if the assignment employee is either between assignments or on vacation and the public holiday therefore does not fall on a regular workday, the assignment employee will only be entitled to public holiday pay, not to an additional day or any of the other public holiday entitlements (note that prior to the 2009 changes to the Act, assignment employees would generally not be entitled to any public holiday entitlements in such a situation); and
- an assignment employee who provides professional services, personal support care or homemaking services under the *Home Care and Community Services Act, 1994* for an employer under contract within the *Community Care Access Corporations Act, 2001* is exempt from the new temporary help agencies section of the Act and is therefore entitled to all of the usual public holiday entitlements described below.

The Act provides that employees are entitled to a day off with public holiday pay on days designated as public holidays.

There are nine public holidays in Ontario:

1.   New Year's Day (January 1);
2.   Family Day (third Monday in February);
3.   Good Friday (Friday before Easter Sunday, which is always between March 22 and April 25);
4.   Victoria Day (Monday before May 25);
5.   Canada Day (July 1, unless July 1 falls on a Sunday, on which the public holiday will be July 2)
6.   Labour Day (first Monday in September);
7.   Thanksgiving Day (second Monday in October);
8.   Christmas Day (December 25); and
9.   Boxing Day (December 26).

To qualify for the day off with public holiday pay, the employee must work the last regularly scheduled work day before the public holiday and the first regularly scheduled work day following the public holiday unless the employee has reasonable cause for failing to do so. For example, if an employee has regular shifts on Wednesday, Thursday and Saturday and the public holiday falls on a Monday, the employee must work his or her entire shift on the Saturday before the public holiday and his or her entire shift on the Wednesday following the public holiday to qualify.

Depending on the situation, an employee who does work on a public holiday is entitled to either "premium pay" or "public holiday pay". Premium pay is pay at least one and one half times an employee's regular rate.

Public holiday pay is calculated based upon the concept of a work week. A work week is a seven-day week selected by the employer. If the employer does not select a work week, then the work week begins Sunday and ends Saturday. To calculate public holiday pay, a company adds the regular wages and vacation pay payable to the employee in the four work weeks before the work week in which the public holiday falls, and then divides by 20. For example, if the employer has selected Tuesday to Monday as the work week and the public holiday falls on Monday, December 25, the four work weeks used in the calculation begin on Tuesday, November 21 and end on Monday, December 18. Add the employee's regular wages and paid vacation pay for that period and divide by 20 to get the public holiday pay entitlement. Regular wages for public holiday pay calculation purposes do not include overtime or premium pay payable to an employee, but do include vacation paid during the calculation period.

For temporary help employees (assignment employees), the calculation for public holiday pay is based on an average of all regular wages and vacation pay earned in the four-week period prior to the public holiday, regardless of the number of assignments to which the agency sent the employee.

If the public holiday falls on a day that would ordinarily be a working day for the employee, and the employee is not on vacation that day, the company has three options:

(1)   the employee may take the day off with public holiday pay;

(2)   the employee may work on the public holiday at the regular rate and take another working day off with public holiday pay; or

(3)   the employee may work on the public holiday at a premium rate for each hour worked plus be paid public holiday pay for the day. The employee is not entitled to another day off work.

The employee is entitled to option (1); however, options (2) and (3) must be agreed upon by the employer and employee in writing. Note the exceptions described above regarding temporary help employees (assignment employees).

If the public holiday falls on a day during the employee's vacation, the company has four options:

(1)   the employee may take another day off that would ordinarily be a working day and receive public holiday pay for that day;

(2)   the employee may receive public holiday pay for the public holiday;

(3)   the employee may work on the public holiday at the regular rate, take another day off that would ordinarily be a working day and receive public holiday pay for that day; or

(4)   the employee may work on the public holiday at a premium rate for each hour worked plus be paid public holiday pay for the day. The employee is not entitled to another day off work.

The employee is entitled to option (1); however, options (2), (3) and (4) may be agreed upon by the employer and employee in writing.

A day substituted for a public holiday must be a day no more than three months after the public holiday for which it was earned unless the employer and employee agree in writing to it being within 12 months. For the purposes of calculating public holiday pay where a substitute day has been agreed upon, the four work week calculation period is that period before the work week in which the substitute day falls.

Special rules apply for employees employed in continuous operations, in a hospital or in the hospitality industry. In such cases, employers can require the employee to work a public holiday and either:

(1) pay the employee the regular rate for each hour worked and schedule another regular working day to be the public holiday with pay; or

(2) pay the employee time and one-half for hours worked and public holiday pay.

Retail Businesses

In most retail businesses employees have the right to refuse to work either a public holiday or on a Sunday unless they agreed to work on Sundays when they were hired. Such agreements to work Sundays can be set aside for religious reasons if they violate the *Human Rights Code*.

Retail establishments must also consider the *Retail Business Holidays Act*, which prohibits operating on nine designated holidays. Eight of these holidays are the same as in the *Employment Standards Act* but in place of December 26 is Easter Sunday. A municipality can pass a by-law exempting businesses within its boundaries from the *Retail Business Holidays Act*. The City of Toronto has passed such a by-law.

Shops can therefore generally open on Boxing Day but must apply the requirements of the *Employment Standards Act*. Local by-laws can require shops to close on Boxing Day.

There are several exemptions to the general operating prohibition in the Act, including:[4]

- shops whose only goods offered for sale are foodstuffs, tobacco and tobacco supplies, antiques or handicrafts, so long as no more than three persons are engaged in selling at any one time and the establishment is less than 2,400 square feet in size;
- pharmacies, so long as prescriptions are available and the premises are not more than 7,500 square feet;

---

[4] This is not a complete list.

- vendors of gasoline, motor oil and motor vehicle supplies;
- nurseries and flower shops;
- fresh fruit and vegetable vendors from April 1 to November 30;
- book, newspaper and periodical sellers, and art galleries, so long as no more than three people are involved in selling at any one time and the establishment is less than 2,400 square feet in size;
- licensed liquor stores;
- educational, recreational and amusement operations incidentally selling goods or services related to such activities.

VACATIONS

As noted above, "public holidays" and "vacations" are separate concepts in the Act. A discussion of public holidays is in the previous section.

The entitlement to time off for vacation and to vacation pay are separate calculations under the Act. Employers who give time off with pay are usually, but not always, in strict compliance.

The exemptions set out in "list one" under "Hours of Work" above apply to the vacation entitlements, other than for information technology professionals, who are eligible for vacation entitlements. The remainder of the exemptions discussed above for other standards do not apply. For example, managers and supervisors are not exempt from the vacation requirement and are therefore entitled to vacation entitlements under the Act.

Some employers provide longer service employees with more paid time off than the Act requires. In such cases, the employer may be able to set different rules about vacation provided they result in a greater benefit than the Act.

The Act entitles every employee to at least two weeks of vacation with pay upon completion of each 12 months of employment, whether or not the employment was active employment. Employees on a leave of absence (*i.e.*, parental, pregnancy, disability or emergency) continue to accrue their vacation entitlement during such leaves of absence and are able to defer taking their vacation time until after the leave.

The employer has the right to determine when the employee can take the vacation time, provided that (a) the vacation be completed no later than 10 months after it was earned; and (b) that the vacation time must be granted in a two-week period or two periods of one week each, unless the employee requests in writing to shorter periods, and the employer agrees to the request.

The Act sets out a formula for calculating an employee's vacation time entitlement where vacation time is not taken in complete weeks. In such circumstances, the employee is entitled to the number of days in the employee's regular work week, times two. Therefore, an employee who has a regular work week of four days is entitled to eight days vacation for the year.

However, if an employee does not have a regular work week, the employee is entitled to the average number of days worked per week in the four months preceding the first day of the vacation, times two. Therefore, in order to determine the entitlement for an employee who works irregular work weeks, and who would like to take a vacation, for example, commencing on June 17, the employer:

- adds the number of days worked from February 16 to June 16 inclusive (the previous four months). Assume, for example, the employee worked 49 days in this period;
- determines the number of weeks in that period by dividing the number of days by seven (121 days/7 – 17.29 weeks);
- determines the average number of days worked per week by dividing the number of days by the number of weeks (49 days/17.29 weeks = 2.83 days);
- multiplies by two to get the vacation entitlement for the year (2.83 days × 2 = 5.66).

Employees continue to be entitled to a vacation pay of a minimum of four per cent of the wages earned in the 12 months for which the vacation is given.

The Act requires that vacation pay be paid in a lump sum, before the employee takes the vacation, with three exceptions:

- if the employee is paid by direct deposit or does not take the vacation in complete weeks, the employer may pay vacation pay on the normal pay day for that time;
- if the employee agrees in writing, the employer may pay the vacation pay that accrues during a pay period on the pay day for that period, provided this amount is shown on the employee's wage statements separate from other wages; and
- the employee agrees in writing to any other time for payment of vacation pay.

The Act provides that an employee may be allowed to forego taking vacation time if the Director approves it. It is not yet clear what circumstances may warrant the Director's approval.

There are special rules for employees represented by a trade union who are included in a multi-employer plan. This is typical in the construction industry.

PREGNANCY AND PARENTAL LEAVE PROVISIONS

Both pregnancy leave and parental leave are unpaid leaves provided for under the Act. See the section in Chapter 2 on Employment Insurance for a discussion on when an employee may be entitled to Employment Insurance benefits during pregnancy and parental leave.

Pregnant employees are entitled to take a pregnancy leave of up to 17 weeks of unpaid time off work. To be eligible for pregnancy leave, the employee must have been employed with her employer for at least 13 weeks preceding the expected delivery date of her child.

The employee must normally provide her employer with at least two weeks' written notice before beginning her pregnancy leave. Should she wish to change the date on which she will begin her pregnancy leave, she must normally provide her employer with at least two weeks' written notice. Pregnancy leave must commence within 17 weeks of the expected date of birth of the child and no later than the actual birth date of the child. Usually, pregnancy leave ends 17 weeks after it commenced. An employee who wishes to end her pregnancy leave on a date that is earlier than the preceding dates must provide her employer with at least four weeks' written notice of the new date.

Where medical complications related to the pregnancy result in an employee having to begin the leave earlier than expected, the requirement to give advance notice is set aside. The employer is still entitled to notice that a pregnancy leave has begun and can request medical confirmation of the need for the leave.

Both parents can take a parental leave, including a mother who took a pregnancy leave. In order to qualify for such a leave, an employee must be the "parent" of a child and must have been employed with his or her employer for at least 13 weeks. "Parent" includes a person with whom a child is placed for adoption and a person who is in a relationship of some permanence with a parent of a child and who intends to treat the child as his or her own.

Where the employee has already taken a pregnancy leave, then she is entitled to take a parental leave of up to 35 weeks of unpaid time off work. If the employee did not take a pregnancy leave, then the parental leave can be up to 37 weeks of unpaid time off work. A parental leave must commence no later than 52 weeks after the day the child is born or comes into the employee's custody, care and control for the first time. However, where the employee has taken a pregnancy leave and also wishes to take a parental leave, the parental leave must begin immediately following the pregnancy leave, unless the child has not yet come into her custody, care and control.

An employee must provide his or her employer with at least two weeks' written notice of the date of commencement of a parental leave, and with at least two weeks' written notice of a change in the date of commencement of the parental leave. An exception is provided for where a child arrives earlier than expected. An employee who wishes to end his or her parental leave before the expiry of the 35- or 37-week period, must provide his or her employer with at least four weeks' written notice of the new date.

Rights that Continue During a Leave

An employee who is absent from work on a pregnancy or parental leave continues to participate in pension plans, life insurance plans, accidental death plans, extended health plans, dental plans and any other prescribed plans. During an employee's pregnancy and/or parental leave, an employer must continue to make its contributions with respect to such types of plans, unless the employee gives the employer written notice that he or she does not want to pay his or her contributions, if any. Employees who are on pregnancy or parental leave can also continue to participate in other types of benefit plans if employees who are on other types of leaves are able to continue to participate in those plans.

The period that an employee is absent from work during a pregnancy and/or parental leave must be included for the purposes of calculating his or her length of employment (whether or not it is active or inactive employment); his or her length of service (whether or not it is active or inactive service); and his or her seniority. However, that period is not counted for the purposes of determining whether or not an employee has completed a probationary period.

Upon the conclusion of a pregnancy or parental leave, an employee is entitled to be reinstated to the position he or she most recently held, if it still exists, or to a comparable position if it does not. The reinstated employee must be paid the greater of the most recent wage rate he or she earned with the employer, or the rate that the employee would have earned had he or she worked throughout the leave. Where an employer does not reinstate an employee after her pregnancy/ parental leave, the employer must be prepared to establish that the reasons for the failure to reinstate are unrelated to the employee's leave.

Employees may defer taking any vacation time entitlement until the end of the leave. Vacation pay, however, is still calculated based on actual wages, which in the case of an unpaid leave, may amount to a vacation pay of $0. The entitlement to any vacation pay owing cannot be waived, but the employer and employee can agree to waive some or all of the time off owing or to reschedule when it will be taken.

The creation of combined pregnancy and parental leave to one year mirrored changes to the Employment Insurance system designed to provide benefits to a parent following the birth of a child. A discussion regarding these benefits are found in Chapter 2.

PERSONAL EMERGENCY LEAVE

Employers who regularly employ 50 or more employees must allow their employees to take up to 10 days per calendar year of unpaid personal emergency leave. The 50-employee trigger is determined by including all employees, even if at different locations, of the employer working in Ontario.

Personal emergency leave can be taken for one of three reasons:

(1)   a personal illness, injury or medical emergency;
(2)   the death, illness, injury or medical emergency of a family member; or
(3)   an urgent matter concerning a family member.

Family members for the purposes of such leaves are:

- the employee's spouse or same sex partner;
- a parent, step-parent or foster parent of the employee, the employee's spouse or same sex partner;
- a child, step-child or foster child of the employee, spouse or same sex partner;
- a grandparent, step-grandparent, grandchild or step-grandchild of the employee, spouse or same sex partner;
- the spouse or partner of an employee's child;
- a brother or sister of the employee; or
- a relative of the employee who is dependent on the employee.

The employee is required to notify the employer of his or her plan to take personal emergency leave. Where doing so in advance is not possible, he or she must do so as soon as possible.

A part day leave, for example, for a doctor's appointment, counts fully as one day of the personal emergency leave allowance.

The leave is unpaid, but benefits must be continued during the leave in the same manner as during pregnancy and parental leaves. As well, the rights discussed above that accrue during a pregnancy and parental leave (length of employment, service and seniority; right to be reinstated; and rights regarding wages) apply to a personal emergency leave.

The Employment Standards Branch policy states that employees hired mid-year are entitled to a full 10 days during their first partial year of employment.

FAMILY MEDICAL LEAVE

Employees who expect the imminent death of a close family member are entitled to eight weeks of unpaid family medical leave. This leave can only be taken in periods of entire weeks, not in periods of days.

To be entitled to family medical leave, the employee must advise his or her employer in writing and must produce a certificate from a qualified medical practitioner that states that the close family member faces a significant risk of death within the next 26 weeks.

For the purpose of this leave provision a close family member is:

- the employee's spouse;
- a parent, step-parent or foster parent; or

- a child, step-child or foster child of the employee or the employee's spouse.

Family medical leave is ended by the expiry of the period set out in the medical certificate, or the death of the relative. The employee is entitled to a new leave following the expiry of the certificate period, if a new certificate is issued. An employee's entitlement to family medical leave is in addition to any entitlement under a personal emergency leave (see above).

Where two employees request a leave in regard to the same relative they are entitled to a total of eight weeks combined.

A family medical leave is unpaid, but benefits must be continued during the leave in the same manner as during pregnancy and parental leaves. As well, the rights discussed above that accrue during a pregnancy and parental leave (length of employment, service and seniority; right to be reinstated; and rights regarding wages) apply to a family medical leave.

During this leave, an employee may be entitled to up to six weeks of "compassionate care benefits" under the federal *Employment Insurance Act*. See Chapter 2 for a full discussion on such benefits.

DECLARED EMERGENCIES

An employee is entitled to an unpaid declared emergency leave if he or she cannot work because of an emergency declared under the *Emergency Management and Civil Protection Act* (such as floods, forest fires or a major disease outbreak) or the *Health Protection and Promotion Act* (such as a SARS outbreak or a state imposed medical quarantine).

The length of this leave is for as long as the emergency is declared by an order under the relevant statute.

To be entitled to a declared emergency leave, the employee must advise his or her employer as soon as possible. An employer may require the employee to provide evidence that the declared emergency leave was required.

Declared emergency leave is in addition to any entitlement to a personal emergency leave.

As with each of the above leaves, declared emergency leave is unpaid, but benefits must be continued during the leave in the same manner as during pregnancy and parental leaves. As well, the rights discussed above that accrue during a pregnancy and parental leave (length of employment, service and seniority; right to be reinstated; and rights regarding wages) apply to a declared emergency leave.

ORGAN DONOR LEAVE

An employee who undergoes surgery to donate an organ is entitled to an unpaid organ donor leave of up to 13 weeks. The leave can be extended up to an additional 13 weeks if a legally qualified medical practitioner certifies that the employee requires more time because of the organ donation.

To be eligible for organ donor leave, the employee must be employed with the employer for at least 13 weeks prior to the leave.

An organ donor leave is in addition to any entitlement to a personal emergency leave.

As with each of the above leaves, organ donor leave is unpaid, but benefits must be continued during the leave in the same manner as during pregnancy and parental leaves. As well, the rights discussed above that accrue during a pregnancy and parental leave (length of employment, service and seniority; right to be reinstated; and rights regarding wages) apply to an organ donor leave.

RESERVIST LEAVE

An employee is entitled to a reservist leave if he or she is deployed to an international Canadian Forces operation or to a national Canadian Forces operation that provides assistance in dealing with an emergency or its aftermath.

To be eligible for reservist leave, the employee must have been employed by the employer for at least six consecutive months. The length of a reservist leave is for as long as the Canadian Forces operation applies to the employee.

The employee must give reasonable notice to the employer that he or she will require reservist leave, or if that is not possible, the employee must advise the employer of the leave as soon as possible after beginning it.

Reservist leave is unpaid, but unlike the other leaves described above, the employer is not required to continue any benefits for the employee during the leave. The other rights discussed above that accrue during a pregnancy and parental leave (length of employment, service and seniority; right to be reinstated; and rights regarding wages) do apply to a reservist leave. While an employee returning from a reservist leave does have a right to reinstatement, an employer may postpone the employee's reinstatement by two weeks or until the first pay day that falls after the day that the reservist leave ends.

TERMINATION OF EMPLOYMENT

The Act requires that employees be given advance notice before employers terminate their employment. Where working notice is not given, pay in lieu of notice is required. Pay in lieu of notice must be paid as a lump sum and the employer must continue all insured benefits for what should have been the notice period. It may also be possible to assign the employee to merely be available at home during the notice period (the British call this "garden leave").

The length of notice required for an individual termination is determined by an employee's length of service as follows:

Length of Service	Notice Requirement
3 months but less than 1 year	1 week
1 year but less than 3 years	2 weeks
3 years but less than 4 years	3 weeks
4 years but less than 5 years	4 weeks
5 years but less than 6 years	5 weeks
6 years but less than 7 years	6 weeks
7 years but less than 8 years	7 weeks
8 years or more	8 weeks

Employees who had a break in employment will have all their service counted unless the break exceeded 13 weeks. Furthermore, any time spent on a statutory leave or other type of inactive employment must be included in determining an employee's length of service.

Where 50 or more employees are being terminated in any four-week period, special "mass termination" provisions will apply. Employees in a mass termination are all entitled to the same amount of notice. The required notice period varies with the number being terminated:

Number of Employees	Notice Requirement
50-199	8 weeks
200-499	12 weeks
500 or more	16 weeks

The statutory notice period for mass terminations does not start to run until the Ministry of Labour receives a disclosure statement outlining, among other things, the following:

- the consultative process — involving the employer, employees and the community — intended or in place to deal with the terminations;
- the economic circumstances surrounding the terminations;
- a statistical profile of each employee involved noting age, sex, occupation, length of service, *etc.*;
- proposed adjustment programs to aid affected employees;
- the locations involved;
- the number of employees at each location, the number being terminated, and whether they are hourly or salaried; and
- the expected termination date.

In instances, where 10 per cent or less of the employees in an establishment are being terminated for reasons other than permanent discontinuance of part of the operations, only the individual notice requirement applies.

The notice of termination requirements do not apply to the following employees (however, some of the following may be included in the count to determine whether the "mass" termination rules apply):

- employed for a definite term or task for less than one year;
- temporarily laid off (see below);
- who fail to return in reasonable time when recalled;
- guilty of wilful misconduct or disobedience or wilful neglect of duty;
- whose employment has been made impossible by an unforeseeable event, such as the plant burning down;
- employed in the construction industry;
- who refuse offers of reasonable alternative employment with the employer;
- who have reached an established retirement age (but only if the termination would not contravene the *Human Rights Code*);
- who are terminated during a strike or lockout;
- who are engaged in large ship building and repair that have access to supplementary unemployment benefits and that agree to this exemption; or
- who provides professional services, personal support care or homemaking services under the *Home Care and Community Services Act, 1994* for an employer under contract within the *Community Care Access Corporations Act, 2001* and whose arrangement with the employer allows the employee to elect to work or not work when requested by the employer (note that this exemption replaced the former, broader "elect to work" exemption and will be revoked by regulation on October 1, 2012).

A temporary lay-off is defined as a lay-off of not more than 13 weeks in a 20-week period unless the employer continues to make significant payments to, or on behalf of, the employee such as, continuing benefit premium payments or paying supplemental unemployment insurance. Under such a condition, a temporary lay-off can last for up to 35 weeks in a 52-week period.

A temporary lay-off that lasts longer than those limits is regarded as a termination, and the employee will be entitled to termination pay (or pay in lieu of notice). The 35-week limit can be extended by agreement with a union or pursuant to a collective agreement.

An employee with recall rights must be given the choice at the 35-week point of maintaining the recall right or receiving termination pay. An employee who elects to take the termination pay may be required to give up those recall rights. Should the employee elect to retain recall rights, absent agreement with a union, the employer must pay the termination pay to the Director of Employment Standards to be paid to the employee when the recall rights expire or when the employee gives up the recall rights. If the employee is recalled, the money is returned to the employer. Where a union is in place it may agree as to how potential amounts owing are to be held while the lay-off continues.

A notice of termination must be in writing and must be given personally to the employee, mailed by a system that provides verified delivery or by fax or email so long as the employee is equipped to receive such communications.

Special rules apply to employers with seniority systems that allow for bumping rights, as contained in most collective agreements. In such cases, if bumping could result, the employer may post a notice as to who is being terminated, setting out their seniority, job classification and proposed termination date. This notice then becomes notice to anyone bumped.

SEVERANCE PAY

An employer is deemed to have severed the employment of an employee if any of the following occurs:

- the employer dismisses or is unable to continue employing the employee;
- the employer constructively dismisses the employee and in response, the employee resigns within a reasonable period of time;
- the employer lays off the employee for 35 weeks or more in any period of 52 consecutive weeks;
- the employer lays off the employee because of a permanent discontinuation of all of the employer's business at an establishment; or
- the employer gives proper notice of termination and the employee gives the employer written notice at least two weeks before resigning, and that notice of resignation takes effect during the notice period.

In addition to the requirement to provide termination notice or pay in lieu of notice, the employer must also pay severance pay to an employee in any of the above listed circumstances if:

(a)   the employer has an annual payroll in Ontario of at least $2.5 million; and

(b)   the employee has at least five years of service.

Severance pay must also be paid to employees with at least five years of service where over 50 or more employees are terminated within a six-month period as a result of the closure of all or part of the business in Ontario. In such cases, the $2.5 million payroll requirement does not apply.

The amount of severance pay required by legislation is one week's pay per year of service to a maximum of 26 weeks' pay. The formula also provides for partial years of service calculated in completed months (12ths). For example, an employee with 10 and one-half years of service will be entitled to severance pay of 10.5 times his or her weekly wage rate. Unlike termination pay, all periods of employment must be counted, even those followed by a break in employment. However, once severance pay is paid for a particular year of employment, it does not have to be paid again for that year if the employee is re-employed.

In order to meet its severance pay commitments in a manageable fashion, an employer may apply to the Minister of Labour for approval to make payments by instalments over a maximum period of three years.

Disability does not disentitle an employee to pay in lieu of notice or severance pay.

The severance pay entitlement does not apply to the following employees:

- when the close down was caused by the economic consequences of a strike;
- where employment has been made impossible by an unforeseeable event unless it has caused a close down;
- who retire with full retirement benefits;
- who refuse reasonable alternative employment with the employer;
- who are guilty of wilful misconduct or wilful neglect of duty;
- employed in the construction industry or on-site maintenance of buildings, roads, sewers or other works; or
- an employee who provides professional services, personal support care or homemaking services under the *Home Care and Community Services Act, 1994* for an employer under contract within the *Community Care Access Corporations Act, 2001* and whose arrangement with the employer allows the employee to elect to work or not work when requested by the employer (note that this exemption replaced the former, broader "elect to work" exemption and will be revoked by regulation on October 1, 2012).

If employees are first temporarily laid off and then terminated, the period of temporary lay-off is included in determining their severance pay calculation. A period of temporary lay-off preceding a termination is not included in calculating an employee's pay in lieu of notice.

Employees who still have recall rights at the 35-week point may be required to make the same choice of maintaining the right or receiving severance pay as for termination pay (described above).

Other laws and applicable agreements may also affect employment termination including the *Human Rights Code*, contracts of employment, *Labour Relations Act*, *Workplace Safety and Insurance Act* and collective agreements.

SPECIAL TYPES OF EMPLOYMENT

The Act contains specified rules for aspects of certain particular types of employment. These special situations and rules include:[5]

Domestic Workers

The Act specifies maximum room and board allowances that can be applied in determining that minimum wage has been paid. Note that a "domestic worker" is distinguished from a "homemaker", the former of which is employed directly by the householder, while a homemaker must be employed by a person other than the householder.

A separate Act, the *Employment Protection for Foreign Nationals Act (Live-in Caregivers and Others), 2009* introduced special rules for live-in foreign national caregivers who provide child care, senior home support care or the care of a disabled person in the disabled person's home. The statute augments the *Employment Standards Act* and regulates aspects of the employment relationship such as recruiter fees, the requirement to provide the caregiver documents from the Ministry of Labour regarding employee rights, employer record-keeping, and enforcement of complaints.

Homeworkers

Homeworkers are employees who carry out their work mostly in their own residence.

Homeworkers must be paid a minimum wage of 110 per cent of the regular minimum wage. If paid on a piecework basis, as is usually the case, employers must advise employees of the amount being paid per item and of any production requirements.

Records must also be kept showing the name and address of every homeworker and the wages paid to them.

Hospitality Industry/Seasonal Employees

Seasonal employees employed for 24 weeks or less in the hospitality industry, and who are provided room and board, are entitled to overtime premium pay after 50 hours work per week.

---

[5] This is not meant to be a complete list, which is beyond the scope of this publication.

Local Cartage and Highway Transport

Drivers and drivers' helpers employed by companies in the business of transporting goods are entitled to overtime after 50 hours if engaged in local cartage and after 60 hours if engaged in highway transport.

Residential Care Workers

Special hours of work and overtime calculation rules are provided for employees who care for children or developmentally handicapped persons in a family-type residence and who live in the residence.

Temporary Help Agencies

A new section was added to the Act effective November 2009 that addresses "temporary help agencies", their "clients" (*i.e.*, the companies with whom the agency contracts to provide temporary employment) and "assignment employees" (*i.e.*, the temporary employee). The new section introduces a number of new obligations and restrictions for temporary help agencies.

The new provisions also clarify that the temporary help agency remains the employer throughout the assignment of an assignment employee to a client. The agency therefore remains responsible for meeting all applicable employment standards required in the Act, such as payment of wages, hours of work and overtime. See the section above on Public Holidays for the discussion on public holiday entitlements for temporary employees.

The employment relationship begins when the agency agrees to assign or attempts to assign the person to a temporary position with a client or potential client. By this point, the agency must provide to the employee, in writing, the legal name and contact information for the agency. The agency continues to be the employer of the employee during, between and after (until termination) an assignment with a client.

Merely providing a client with a resume, arranging for an interview or introducing the employee to a client does not amount to an assignment. Receiving training from a client for the purpose of performing work with that client will, however, amount to an assignment.

When offering a work assignment to an employee, the agency must provide the employee the following information in writing:

- legal name of the client;
- contact information for the client;
- hourly or other wage rate or commission and any benefits to be paid;
- hours of work;
- general description of the work to be performed;
- pay period and pay day of the agency;

- estimated term of the assignment, if such information is available; and
- a copy of the most recent Ministry of Labour document regarding the rights of temporary workers.

Temporary help agencies are prohibited from charging any fees to an assignment employee for becoming an assignment employee, for arranging any assignments with a client, for preparing resumes or preparing for job interview. The temporary help agency is also prohibited from restricting an assignment employee from entering into direct employment with a client of the agency, or from charging a fee to do so.

Temporary help agencies cannot restrict a client from providing references for an assignment employee or from entering into a direct relationship with an assignment employee.

Essentially the only fee that an agency can now charge a client is when a client and an assignment employee enter into a direct employment relationship, but the fee can only be charged during the first six months of the placement.

Temporary help agencies are now formally required to provide notice of termination or pay in lieu of such notice and, if applicable, severance pay. While many of the regular termination and severance provisions of the Act apply, there are some differences for assignment employees, including:

- how to determine an "excluded week" for the purpose of calculating the number of weeks an employee is on a temporary lay-off;
- the "mass termination" provision, which is triggered if 50 or more assignment employees are terminated at the same client establishment in the same four-week period; and
- the total wages of the 12-week period prior to the last day of work or immediately before the deemed termination date (whichever is greater), divided by 12, are used to calculate termination pay.

EQUAL PAY FOR EQUAL WORK BY MEN AND WOMEN

The provision for equal pay in the *Employment Standards Act* has largely been displaced by the *Pay Equity Act*.

The *Employment Standards Act* requires that men and women be paid the same wages for substantially the same work in the same establishment where substantially the same skills, efforts and responsibilities are involved, and the working conditions are similar.

The equal pay requirement in this Act does not apply if the wage difference is a result of:

- a seniority system;
- a merit system;

- a system where earnings vary with the quantity or quality of production; or
- any other factor other than sex (but note the *Human Rights Code* as well).

In determining whether or not the work is substantially the same, the entire employment and its purpose is considered. In one case where the only difference between male orderlies and female nursing assistants in an old-age home was that the men occasionally did heavy lifting, it was decided that the work was substantially the same.

NO DISCRIMINATION IN BENEFIT PLANS

The Act prohibits discrimination based on age, sex or marital status in regard to any kind of employee benefit plan that provides the employee and the employee's dependants, beneficiaries or survivors with income during retirement or unemployment. Insurance plans covering death, disability, sickness, accident, medical, hospital, dental or other similar benefits are included as well. "Age" for this purpose is defined as over 18 and under 65 years old, thus allowing for different benefit plans for employees over the age of 65.

The regulations exempt differences based on the different life spans of men and women as normally found in life insurance premiums. Also exempt from the non-discrimination rules are:

- benefits that terminate if a surviving spouse remarries;
- pension plan benefits that provide more to married employees;
- minimum age requirements for pension plans;
- pension benefits that vary with the age of the retiree; and
- pension premiums that increase with the age a person enters the plan.

These exemptions and additional similar ones are limited to various specific applications and require complete review if a specific fact situation is being considered.

LIE DETECTOR TESTS

Employers are prohibited from requiring employees or prospective employees to submit to lie detector tests.

This prohibition against lie detector tests is the only part of the *Employment Standards Act* that includes a member or prospective member of a police force.

The Act specifically states, however, that this prohibition in the context of employment does not apply to a person being asked by a police officer to take a lie detector test in Ontario in the course of the investigation of an offence.

SALE OF A BUSINESS

Employee entitlements regarding holidays, vacation with pay, pregnancy leave and notice of termination are all tied to some extent to the length of their service with the employer. The details of these entitlements are outlined in the sections of this chapter regarding these specific topics.

The Act provides that where a business is sold and the purchaser employs the employees of the vendor, the employees maintain their length of service with the new employer. A purchaser should therefore note that employees who remain with the company may have accumulated rights in these areas that the purchaser will have to honour.

Employees being terminated at the time of a sale are entitled to all their usual termination rights as outlined in the section of this chapter on that topic. Note that employees rehired within 13 weeks of a termination are considered to have never been terminated.

When a purchaser agrees to continue the employment of employees, the Employment Standards Branch does not consider the employees terminated by the vendor. However, if the employee refuses the purchaser's offer of employment, the vendor will be treated as having terminated the employee.

Building Service Providers — Business Transfer

Special rules apply where a building service provider is being replaced, although it is not a sale of a business situation. These rules apply to parking garages, concession operations and to property management services. Where a change in operator is occurring, the employees of a predecessor will usually have a right to employment with the successor. The predecessor employer is required to provide to anyone seeking to take over the operation details about its employees, their wages and benefits.

COMPLAINTS, INVESTIGATIONS AND HEARINGS

Employment Standards Officers employed by the Employment Practices Branch investigate complaints by employees not represented by a trade union, carry on general investigations and, when necessary, issue orders requiring compliance with provisions of the Act.

Most investigations result from a complaint to the Branch. Sometimes the investigation resulting from a particular complaint will include other employers in the same industry or the same geographic area in order to help preserve the anonymity of the complainant. Investigations may also result from officers of other government investigatory branches alerting the Employment Standards Branch to a possible breach of their Act. Of course, this cross-alerting goes in both directions.

Officers carrying out investigations are given broad powers under the Act, including the power to:

- enter upon private lands and premises without a warrant (except a private dwelling, in which case, a warrant is required);
- require the production of all books and records and remove them for the purpose of making a copy; and
- ask questions of any individual.

If the officer finds that money is owing, he or she will first see if the matter can be settled voluntarily. If it cannot be settled voluntarily, the officer will issue a written order to pay, which results in an automatic 10 per cent penalty being charged in addition to the amount owing. Generally, an officer's order may not exceed $10,000, however, special circumstances exist, including situations involving pregnancy leave. The officer's order can be filed in court by the Employment Standards Branch and then enforced as if it were a judgment of that court. No court hearing is held.

Violations of the Act can also lead to the officer issuing a notice of contravention.

Where an officer does make an order or issue a notice of contravention, employers have only 30 days to appeal the order to the Ontario Labour Relations Board. In most cases, where the employer has been ordered to pay money, it will have to pay the money to the director in order to appeal the order. If the appeal is successful, the money is returned.

Notices of contravention trigger automatic penalties ranging from $250 to $1,000 where the employer has failed to post information notices as required or has failed to make and retain records as required.

Normally, employees covered by a collective agreement cannot complain to the Branch about a violation of the Act. Instead, such employees must file a grievance as provided for in the collective agreement. In such cases, all rights granted by the Act are considered to be part of the collective agreement. Where the collective agreement contains different, but better, rights then the agreement will prevail.

In certain cases, non-union employees may have the right to pursue an action in the general courts by suing their employer for claims that overlap rights granted by the Act. For example, an employee whose employment has been terminated can sue for wrongful dismissal. In such cases, the employee must choose which remedy to pursue and if suing, the employee cannot also bring a complaint under the Act.

Non-unionized employees may appeal an officer's decision not to issue an order. Such appeals also go to the Ontario Labour Relations Board.

Officers may also issue "tickets" for non-compliance under the *Provincial Offences Act*. Typically, these tickets can amount to hundreds of dollars and they can be appealed to the courts under the Act.

Violations of the Act can also lead to prosecution in the courts. This enforcement route is used when employers make false records, provide misleading information, take action against an employee for making a complaint and also when employers fail to comply with orders made by the officers.

A fine of up to $100,000 (more for subsequent offences) and a jail term of up to 12 months can result from a breach of the general provisions of the Act. In fact, lesser fines are the usual result. Officers, directors and agents of a company can be liable for any action taken by the company if they authorized or permitted the action to take place.

In cases where employees were entitled to a job, such as upon return from pregnancy leave, employers can be ordered to provide the job.

Effective in January 2008, inspectors from one of a number of agencies of the Ontario government will have the authority to involve inspectors from another branch if they are concerned a violation of the other branch's legislation is occurring. In setting penalties, the courts will also be required to consider a company's entire record of regulatory violations.

Finally, the Director of the Employment Standards Branch can order an Ontario Labour Relations Board hearing into allegations that no discrimination rules for benefit plans have been violated. In these cases, there may be no officer's order, instead the matter proceeds directly to the Ontario Labour Relations Board.

Hearings before the Ontario Labour Relations Board, whether initiated by an appeal or by the Director, proceed in a manner similar to a court, with each side presenting its facts and reasons as to why it should win. Depending upon the importance of the issues and the location of the hearing, the Branch will be represented either by an officer or by a lawyer from the Ministry of Labour. Employers and employees have the right to be represented by lawyers as well.

Where a matter is scheduled to proceed to a hearing before the Ontario Labour Relations Board, the Board may appoint one of its officers to try and assist the parties in reaching a settlement.

DIRECTOR LIABILITY

Corporate Directors may be personally liable for up to six months of the employees' wages in certain circumstances where the corporate employer does not pay the employees. This liability does not apply to directors of most non-profit corporations.

INFORMATION POSTINGS

Employers are required to post a copy of a poster prepared by the Ministry of Labour called "What You Should Know About the Ontario *Employment Standards Act*". The poster must be posted in English and, if another language is that of the majority of the workplace, in such other language, if a translation is available from the Ministry. As of summer 2010, the poster was available in 23 languages.

Where an appeal of an order is made to the Labour Board, the Board has the authority to order notices regarding the process to be posted.

Chapter 2

Further Minimum
Terms of Employment

HUMAN RIGHTS AND PROHIBITED DISCRIMINATION

Discrimination Prohibited

The Ontario *Human Rights Code* (the "Code") guarantees people equal treatment regardless of their race, ancestry, place of origin, colour, ethnic origin, citizenship, creed, sex, sexual orientation, age, record of offences, marital status, family status or disability in regard to their employment and the opportunity for employment. It also guarantees these protections in their right to contract and in regard to the provision of services, goods, facilities and residential accommodation.

Discrimination in providing accommodation because a person is in receipt of public assistance is also prohibited. Finally, sexual harassment of employees is prohibited.

The Code is considered to be a quasi-constitutional piece of legislation and most employers in Ontario are bound by its requirements.

While some of the prohibited grounds of discrimination are self-explanatory, others require some elaboration:

(i) **Age.** Age is defined as meaning over 18, so it is permissible to discriminate in employment regarding those below 18. It is not discrimination where an age of 65 or over is a requirement, qualification or consideration for preferential treatment. For example, the Code allows for pension funds and employee insurance funds to make distinctions based on age to the same extent such distinctions are allowed by the *Employment Standards Act* (see section on "No Discrimination in Benefit Plans" in Chapter 1). Admittance to employment cannot be denied, however, because an employee may not qualify for one of these benefits.

(ii) **Disability.** Disability is broadly defined and includes any actual or perceived degree of physical disability, a condition of mental impairment or developmental disability, a learning disability or a mental disorder. The definition of disability also includes "an injury or disability for which benefits were claimed or received under the insurance plan established under the *Workplace Safety and Insurance Act, 1997*". Employers can refuse to employ a disabled person only if the disability makes the person incapable of performing the "essential duties" of the job. In other words, it is not acceptable to point to an occasional function that could be done by someone else or that does not really belong to the job in question. The Code requires an employer to accommodate an employee with disabilities up to "undue hardship". The "undue hardship" of an employer is a high threshold. Factors to consider when determining whether an employer has sufficiently attempted to accommodate a disabled employee are the cost, any outside sources of funding and health and safety requirements. Some cost or a mere inconvenience to either the employer or to co-employees will not amount to "undue hardship". Reasonable, good faith distinctions are allowed in the treatment of employees with a pre-existing disability who are in a disability plan where there are either fewer than 25 employees or where the entire premium is employee paid. Where the employer pays the premiums for a plan that a disabled employee cannot join, an amount equal to the per-employee premium must be paid to the disabled employee. A special problem arises where disabled people are discriminated against because of the design of certain facilities or premises. Again, the Code provides that an employer may be ordered to redesign such premises or facilities unless the cost of doing so would cause an "undue hardship" to the employer.

(iii) **Marital Status.** The marital status ground applies to the status of being married, single, widowed, divorced or separated. It also includes the status of living with a person in a conjugal relationship outside of marriage (a "common-law relationship"). Equal protections apply to both same-sex and opposite-sex relationships.

(iv) **Certain Offences.** Discrimination based on an offence under any provincial enactment or based on a pardoned criminal offence is prohibited.

(v) **Family Status.** The prohibition applies to discrimination based on a parent-child relationship and includes non-biological relationships such as adopted children, step-children or foster children, as well as non-biological children of gay or lesbian parents.

(vi) **Pregnancy.** The prohibition applies to discrimination because a woman is or may become pregnant.

Exceptions

Employers are allowed to consider age, sex, record of offences and marital status where such matters are good faith job qualifications.

Presumably, this would allow employers to consider traffic violations in hiring a truck driver and to consider gender in hiring a washroom attendant.

Religious, charitable, educational, and social organizations may discriminate on any of the prohibited grounds where the otherwise prohibited qualification is a good faith requirement because of the nature of the organization.

Persons employing someone to look after the medical or personal needs of a person in a private household are completely exempt.

The Code also allows an employer to implement special programs designed to relieve hardship or economic disadvantage or to assist disadvantaged persons or groups to achieve equal opportunity. Called "equal opportunity programs", such schemes often promote the hiring, training and promotion of classes of people who have historically, for various reasons, not enjoyed equal treatment. In the United States such programs are often mandatory for African Americans. In Canada, they are most often discussed in relation to women, but also apply to visible minorities, native peoples and the disabled.

Employment Application Forms

Employment application forms, interview questions and hiring procedures generally must comply with the Code.

For example, application forms cannot ask:

- the legal basis for being able to work in Canada (the form can only ask whether the applicant is legally able to do so); and
- the name and location of elementary schools as this may discriminate on the basis of race, ancestry, place of origin, colour, citizenship, creed, *etc.* (though such questions about secondary schools and more senior institutions are permitted).

Sexual Harassment

As well as prohibiting discrimination on sexual grounds, the Code also prohibits any person in authority from making sexual advances where that person knows or ought to know that the advances are unwelcome.

This section would clearly apply to an employer-employee relationship as well as to all senior-junior employee relationships within a company.

Any person who had the authority to stop the conduct in question, for example, a more senior person in management, and who knew or ought to have known about it, can be made a party to a complaint about sexual harassment.

Complaints, Investigations and Hearings

As of July 1, 2009, complaints of a violation of the Code are brought before the Human Rights Tribunal. The previous role of the Human Rights Commission as gatekeeper and advocate to initiate its own complaints has been eliminated. The Human Rights Commission no longer has the authority to resolve or investigate human rights complaints. Its role continues to focus on public education, policy development and research, and includes the ability to conduct public inquiries. The Human Rights Commission can also intervene in Human Rights Tribunal proceedings or initiate its own applications at the Human Rights Tribunal, but it no longer represents individuals in such proceedings.

Persons wishing to file an application (formerly called a "complaint") at the Human Rights Tribunal can now do so directly, without the intervention of the Human Rights Commission. Applicants can obtain assistance with their application from the Human Rights Legal Support Centre, an independent agency funded by the Ontario government. Respondents, which in the employment law context are most often the employer, cannot access the Centre, but will find a number of resources on the Human Rights Commission and the Human Rights Tribunal websites.

Proceedings before the Human Rights Tribunal are becoming increasingly legalistic and formal. The Code, Rules of Procedure, Practice Directions, Policies, Guides and relevant decisions should all be reviewed before appearing before the Human Rights Tribunal. Most of these documents are available on the Human Rights Tribunal website, online: <http://www.hrto.ca>.

If the Tribunal finds that the Code has been violated, it has extensive power not only to award damages (the payment of money), including damages for mental anguish, but also, to order that action be taken to remedy the complaint and ensure future compliance, including reinstatement to employment or a hiring. The Tribunal can order an employer to employ a person if it is determined that the person was refused employment in violation of the Code.

The decision of the Tribunal may be appealed to the Divisional Court.

Allegations of a violation of the Code may also be made as part of an action in the courts, typically for "wrongful dismissal" (see Chapter 5).

Government Contracts and Grants

The Code contains a special provision allowing for the government to cancel any contract with, or any grant, loan or guarantee to, a person or company found by the Tribunal to have violated the Code.

EMPLOYMENT INSURANCE

Who is Covered?

The *Employment Insurance Act* is federal legislation which applies to all Ontario employers. Formerly known as Unemployment Insurance, it was renamed in 1996 as part of a revision of the system, and is now generally referred to as "EI benefits".

EI benefits are designed to provide income protection for employees who are unemployed for various reasons. A limited number of employees are not covered by the *Employment Insurance Act*. The most common exclusions are:

(a)   persons employed on a casual basis to do work not directly connected to the employer's business (for example, a person who serves food at a company picnic but is not otherwise employed);

(b)   a spouse or other dependant of the employer where the parties are not at arm's length;

(c)   a person employed by a corporation who controls more than 40 per cent of the voting shares;

(d)   persons who exchange their work or services for the work or services of someone else; and

(e)   a person employed in agriculture or horticulture who is not paid or who works less than seven days per year with the same employer.

Special rules apply to fishers, taxi drivers, barbers and hairdressers. Information regarding these rules are available from the Service Canada website, online: <http://www.servicecanada.gc.ca/eng/sc/ei/index.shtml> and the Canada Revenue Agency website, online: <http://www.cra-arc.gc.ca/tx/bsnss/tpcs/pyrll/clcltng/ei/menu-eng.html>.

Self-Employed Persons

Starting in January 2010, self-employed persons can opt in and pay EI premiums on a voluntary basis in order to qualify for the following EI benefits: maternity, parental, sickness and compassionate care benefits. Such persons will be able to make a claim for the four types of EI benefits as of January 2011.

A "self-employed person" is defined as someone who operates his or her own business or someone who is employed by a corporation but is not eligible to participate in the EI program as an employee because he or she controls more than 40 per cent of the voting shares of that corporation.

To be eligible to make a claim in 2011, the self-employed person must make a minimum income of $6,000 in 2010. The EI premium rate for self-employed persons is the same as the employee rate, which in 2010 is $1.73 per $100 of earnings (up to a yearly maximum of $43,200).

Insurable Earnings

Effective January 1, 2010, wages earned by employees, unless they are exempt, are insured by the EI benefits program yearly to a maximum amount of $43,200. Certain amounts are specifically included in the earnings calculation, including:

(a)   bonuses and gratuities;

(b)   profit shares;

(c)   accumulative overtime settlements, sick leave credits, awards or vacation pay;

(d)   severance pay or termination pay ("wages in lieu of notice");

(e)   retirement benefits and leave;

(f)   room and board; and

(g)   back pay awarded on a reinstatement to work.

Not included are:

(a)   payments under a supplemental unemployment benefit plan as sometimes found in collective agreements; and

(b)   directors' fees.

Premiums

Both the employer and the employee contribute to the EI benefits program. The employer is required to remit the employer premiums, as well as to deduct and remit employee premiums.

For 2010, the employee premium rate is 1.73 per cent of insurable earnings and the premium rate for employers is 1.4 times the employee rate (2.42 per cent in 2010). The premium is deducted from each dollar earned, up to the maximum yearly insurable earnings, which is $43,200 in 2010.

Tables and general information on payroll deductions for EI benefits are available from the Canada Revenue Agency website, online: <http://www.cra-arc.gc.ca/tx/bsnss/tpcs/pyrll/clcltng/ei/menu-eng.html>.

Illness Insurance Premium Reduction

A reduction in the employer's premium rate is available to employers who provide a system, usually insurance, that duplicates EI benefits payable to employees who are absent as a result of sickness or pregnancy.

The reduction in rate becomes effective in the second full year that the employer offers such a plan.

In order to qualify for the reduction the employer's system must meet extensive and specific tests, the most important of which are:

(a)   the benefit waiting period must not exceed 14 days;

(b)   the benefits must be payable for at least 15 weeks;

(c)   the benefit payable must be at least equal to the amount of benefits the employee would receive from the EI program; and

(d)   the employee must be eligible to claim benefits under the plan within three continuous months of starting employment with the employer.

Information describing the requirements to obtain this deduction is available from the Service Canada website, online: <http://www.servicecanada.gc.ca/eng/cs/prp/0200_000.shtml>.

Insurance companies offering wage-protection insurance have packages designed to trigger the reduction.

Terminating Employees

When an employee covered by the EI benefits program is terminated from employment, the employer is required to complete a "Record of Employment" form supplied by Service Canada.

If filing a paper version of the form, the employer must forward a copy of the form to the employee and send in a paper version of the form to Service Canada within five calendar days of termination.

If filing the form electronically, the employer is no longer required to provide a copy to the employee, but must file the form with Service Canada within five calendar days after the end of the regular pay period (or within 15 days of termination if the pay period is monthly or longer).

These rules apply to employees whose earnings are being stopped for any reason, including illness and pregnancy.

Work-Sharing Agreements

Work-sharing is a federal program designed to assist workplaces that are experiencing a reduction in business levels of at least 10 per cent that is beyond the control of the employer. The purpose of the program is to avoid temporary lay-offs by providing employees with EI benefits during the reduced employment period.

Such programs must be agreed upon between the employer and employee (or, if applicable, the union) and be approved by Service Canada.

There are a number of specific criteria and there is an extensive application process that the employer must go through to qualify. If approved, the employer can reduce the amount of work activity between 20-60 per cent, while eligible employees will be entitled to receive EI benefits for the days off.

Information is available on the Service Canada website, online: <http://www.servicecanada.gc.ca/eng/work_sharing/index.shtml>.

Maternity and Parental Benefits

EI benefits are available for parents during a maternity and/or parental leave (see the discussion in Chapter 1 regarding the entitlement to time off for a pregnancy and/or parental leave).

An employee who is the birth mother or surrogate mother of a newborn child is entitled to 15 weeks of maternity EI benefits.

A female or male employee who is the parent of a newborn or who adopts a child is entitled to collect parental EI benefits for 35 weeks after the arrival of the child, within the 52 weeks following the child's birth or the date the adopted child is placed with the parent. Either of the parents is eligible for the benefits, and the total of 35 weeks may be shared by the two parents.

For a birth or surrogate mother, this could be an additional 35 weeks of EI benefits.

The amount of EI benefits to which an employee is entitled during a maternity and/or parental leave will be the same amount as the regular EI benefits described in the "Benefits" section below.

Compassionate Care Benefits

Employees who must temporarily take time off work to care for a gravely ill family member who is at significant risk of death within 26 weeks may be entitled to compassionate care EI benefits.

Compassionate care EI benefits provide EI benefits for a total of six weeks and can be shared with other family members.

To be eligible for this EI benefit, the employee must have worked at least 600 hours in the last 52 weeks, and are required to provide appropriate medical documentation. This EI benefit may be combined with other EI benefits, such as maternity or parental EI benefits.

Sickness Benefits

Up to 15 weeks of sickness EI benefits may be paid to employees who are unable to work because of sickness, injury or quarantine.

To be eligible, employees must have worked at least 600 hours in the last 52 weeks, and are required to provide appropriate medical documentation. This EI benefit may be combined with other EI benefits, such as maternity or parental EI benefits.

Amount of Benefits

Unless an employee is disentitled or disqualified, he or she will be entitled to a weekly EI benefit of 55 per cent of his or her average weekly insurable earnings, up to the maximum yearly insurable amount. In 2010, this amounted to a maximum payment of $457 per week.

To qualify for EI benefits, an employee must normally have worked a minimum number of hours in the last 52 weeks, referred to as the "qualifying period". Employees who have previously been receiving benefits or who have been ill may have different qualifying periods amounts. The minimum number of hours in the qualifying period ranges from 420 to 700 hours and varies from place to place across Canada, depending on the local unemployment rate. (Information is available from the Service Canada website, online: <http:// www.servicecanada.gc.ca/eng/ei/types/regular.shtml#Number>.

A two-week waiting period exists before benefits commence and employees cannot earn normal wages during the waiting periods.

Benefits normally last up to 50 weeks for persons who have been fully employed and have not recently received a benefit under the EI benefits scheme; this period may vary depending on local unemployment rates. Sickness and maternity benefits last up to 15 weeks, parental benefits up to 35 weeks and compassionate care benefits up to six weeks.

For unemployed persons, benefits are paid only if the person is available for work. Normally, this requires that they regularly seek work and maintain regular contact with Service Canada. This rule does not apply to persons seeking benefits as a result of sickness, maternity, parental leave or compassionate care leave.

Persons out of work because of a labour dispute (*e.g.*, strike or lockout) at their workplace are not entitled to EI benefits.

Persons who quit their jobs without just cause or are fired for misconduct can be denied EI benefits completely.

Where an employee is paid severance pay or pay in lieu of notice, EI payments are delayed. The severance payment is divided by the regular weekly wage to determine the number of weeks the payment is worth, and EI benefits are not paid during such weeks. At the end of these weeks, EI benefits may be applied for.

Persons who feel they have not received an EI benefit they are entitled to should contact the local office of Service Canada. If the failure to receive the EI benefit is because of the decision of an EI agent at a Service Canada Centre, such decisions may be appealed within 30 days.

Social Insurance Numbers

Employees require a Social Insurance Number to access government services such as EI benefits.

Employers are required to obtain an employee's Social Insurance Number within three days of their commencing work. If no number is available, they must report this to the local Service Canada office. Employees who have not previously obtained a card must immediately apply for one and show it to the employer within three days of receiving it.

The Service Canada website has the information and required application forms describing the application procedure.

WORKERS' COMPENSATION

Compulsory Insurance — No Civil Suits

The *Workplace Safety and Insurance Act* (the "WSIA") provides a compulsory Ontario workplace insurance scheme which makes compensation available to an employee injured while at work. A disability due to industrial disease can also result in compensation being paid.

Employers covered by the WSIA must pay into an Insurance Fund maintained by the Workers Safety and Insurance Board (the "WSIB"). Employees make no payments and deductions from employees to cover payments are prohibited.

The employer's financial return for participation is security from being sued. The WSIA prohibits any employee covered by the scheme from suing his or her employer or any other covered employer because of an accident occurring while the employee is at work.

Coverage

The WSIA specifically sets out a long list of types of operations to which it applies. Virtually all manufacturing and construction employers are covered, as are operators of hospitals, hotels, restaurants, theatres, security services and land surveying businesses. Farming operations are also covered, as are domestic workers such as housekeepers, maids, nannies, chauffeurs and gardeners. Employers not compulsorily covered may apply to the WSIB to come under the WSIA. Certain very large employers are excluded from contributing to the Insurance Fund and are required to self-insure. These employers include railways, telephone companies, shipping lines and international airlines.

Contributions

The required amount of employer contribution is calculated on a payroll basis and varies from industry to industry. In 2010, the average assessment was approximately $2.26 per $100 of payroll.

The contribution level may be increased by the WSIB for employers with a poor accident record.

Contribution details for a specific industry or employer can be obtained from the WSIB and its website, online: <http://www.wsib.on.ca>.

Accident Procedures

Employers are required to report to the WSIB all accidents that require medical attention, beyond first aid, or that result in loss of time in excess of the day of the accident. Such reports must be submitted within three days of the accident. Records must also be kept of all minor accidents requiring first aid even if a report is not necessary. Employees and doctors treating employees injured at work are also required to file reports with the WSIB.

Forms are available from the WSIB for the required reports.

If there is any dispute about an employee's entitlement to compensation, the WSIB has its own staff to gather additional information before an initial decision is made by the administrative staff.

First Aid Requirements

The WSIA and regulations require that employers maintain a first aid station. At the station the employer must post the WSIB's poster regarding treatment of injuries and maintain various first aid supplies.

The design of the station and the types of supplies required varies with the size of the workforce and is detailed in the regulations.

For example, employers with less than five employees are required to have a box containing the current edition of a standard St. John Ambulance First Aid Manual and various bandage supplies. Employers with over 200 employees must have a first aid room with a full range of equipment and furnishings. Details of these requirements are available from the WSIB in its publication called "First Aid Requirements", which is available for download from the WSIB website, online: <http://www.wsib.on.ca/files/content/DownloadableFile FirstAidRequirementsreg1011/FAEng.pdf>.

All employers are required to have at least one employee who has first aid training from an agency recognized by the Board. The number of employees who must be certified and the type of certificate required varies with the size of the workforce.

Employers are also required to provide an injured employee with transportation to a hospital, doctor or to the employee's home, whichever is required after the accident.

Employee Benefits

1. **Basic Benefit for Loss of Earnings.** Employees whose employers are covered by the WSIA are entitled to compensation for losses resulting from an injury that occurs in the course of their employment. Compensation is also available because of certain illnesses resulting from the employee's work environment.

Generally, in the case of accidents, compensation for lost earnings starts the day after the accident.

When an employer continues an employee's pay while the employee is absent due to injury, the employer is entitled to reimbursement from the Insurance Fund. Such payments are subject to the maximum that the employee would have received.

Under the WSIA, the spouse of an employee who has died from a workplace injury or disease is entitled to: (1) a lump-sum payment (in 2010, this payment is $71,984.30 plus or minus $1,799.61 for each year the spouse is under/over the age of 40, respectively); (2) continuing monthly payments for both the spouse and children based on the deceased employee's pre-injury net wage up to a set maximum earnings ceiling; and (3) the cost of expenses related to the burial. The calculation of the amount of the first two payments is dependent upon the age of the surviving spouse. If the surviving spouse receives survivor's benefits under the Canada Pension Plan, the amount so received will be deducted from the average earnings of the deceased employee for the purposes of calculating the periodic payment in (2) above.

The scheme is a no-fault system and so an employee's own negligence does not disentitle him or her to benefits. However, where the accident is caused by the employee's own "serious and wilful" misconduct, benefits will be denied unless the accident is serious. In practice, an accident is considered serious if the employee is away from work for longer than six weeks.

The amount of benefit paid for a total but temporary disability is 85 per cent of the employee's net average earnings subject to a maximum that is indexed according to a unique formula in the WSIA. If the disability is temporary and allows continued employment, a reduced payment is made.

Where a permanent disability results, the payment is based on the degree of impairment to the employee's earnings ability. The maximum is 85 per cent of the employee's net average earnings up to an earning ceiling that is regularly revised. Minimum benefits are also provided for. Benefits are tax free.

An employee who is able to resume employment but fails to do so can have his or her benefits reduced or cancelled by the WSIB.

2. **Non-Economic Loss.** Benefits for a "non-economic loss" are intended to compensate an employee for the physical, functional or psychological loss caused by an impairment. In order to receive benefits for non-economic loss, an employee must suffer "permanent impairment". Employees who are temporarily disabled will not be entitled to benefits for non-economic loss. The term "permanent" is defined in the WSIA to mean "impairment that continues to exist after the employee reaches maximum medical recovery". "Impairment" in turn, is defined to mean any "physical or functional abnormality or loss (including disfigurement) which results from an injury and any psychological damage arising from the abnormality or loss".

3. **Health Care Benefits.** Health care benefits will continue to be provided. However, the WSIA lists the types of health care which will be available. Injured employees will be required to cooperate in the health care measure that the WSIB considers appropriate, and failure to do so may result in the reduction or suspension of benefit payments. Health care professionals are also required to provide the WSIB and employers with such information concerning the employees' functional abilities as is set out in the regulations.

Return to Work

Employers and employees both have obligations to cooperate in the early and safe return of employees to work. An employer must contact, and maintain contact, with an employee as soon as possible after injury. It must attempt to identify and arrange suitable employment that is consistent with the employee's functional abilities, and restore the employee's pre-injury earnings. Employees must cooperate with the employer in all of these measures.

The WSIB will contact the parties to provide assistance where necessary. Assistance may include facilitating consultation and communication between the employer and employee; the resolution of disputes; or guidance in the creation of workplace-based return-to-work programs.

Work Reintegration Programs

Where an employee has been unable to return to work with the pre-injury employer, and has cooperated in all return-to-work and recovery measures, the WSIB will conduct an assessment to determine whether "a worker requires a labour market re-entry plan in order to enable the worker to re-enter the labour market and reduce or eliminate the loss of earnings that may result from the injury" (s. 42(2)). The plan will be developed by the WSIB with input from the employee, the employer and the employee's health professional. This process has replaced the vocational rehabilitation services formerly offered by the WSIB.

Appeals Tribunal

If employees, survivors or employers disagree with a decision of the WSIB, they may file an objection, generally within six months after the decision. A notice of objection must set out why the decision is incorrect. The WSIB will provide mediation services to help the parties resolve disagreements themselves, in addition to conducting traditional hearings.

To appeal a decision of the WSIB, employees, survivors or employers must file an appeal with the Workplace Safety and Insurance Appeals Tribunal ("WSIAT"). WSIAT is an independent tribunal that is separate from the WSIB.

The jurisdiction of WSIAT is restricted to appeals from a final decision of the WSIB with respect to entitlement to health care; return to work; labour market re-entry; entitlement to other benefits; an employer's classification under the insurance plan; and the amounts of premiums and penalties payable by an employer.

Obligation to Reinstate Employees

The WSIA requires employers to reinstate employees following recovery from work-related injuries.

This provision does not apply to:

(a) employers and employees engaged in the construction industry;

(b) employers who regularly employ fewer than 20 employees; and

(c) classes of employment exempted by regulation.

In order for an employee to be able to take advantage of the provision, he or she must have been continuously employed with the employer for at least one year on the date of injury. Where the employee qualifies, the employer must:

(i) reinstate the employee to the position he or she held on the date of injury, or provide the employee with alternative employment of a nature and at earnings comparable to the employee's employment on that date; or

(ii) where the employee is unable to perform the essential duties of a position described in (i), offer the employee the first opportunity to accept suitable employment that may become available with the employer.

The above obligation lasts until the earliest of:

(1) two years after the date of injury to the employee;

(2) one year after the date the employee is able to return to the pre-injury employment; and

(3) the date the employee reaches the age of 65.

Where an employer reinstates an employee and then terminates the employment within six months, the employer is presumed to have breached the reinstatement obligation unless it can prove the contrary. Where an employer fails to comply with the section, it is subject to a penalty equal to the employee's net average earnings for the year preceding the injury, subject to the income ceilings in place. In such circumstances, the WSIB has the authority to make temporary disability payments to the employee for a maximum period of one year.

Where the reinstatement obligation conflicts with a provision under a collective agreement, the *Workplace Safety and Insurance Act* governs to the extent that it provides a greater benefit. However, the reinstatement obligation does not operate to displace the seniority provisions of a collective agreement.

When determining whether or how to reinstate an employee, both the WSIA and the *Human Rights Code* require an employer to accommodate the employee up to undue hardship.

Maintenance of Employment Benefits

Employers who contribute to employees' pension and health-related employment benefits at the time of injury must continue to do so during such employee's absence up to a maximum of one year following the date of injury, so long as the employee continues to pay his or her share, if any, for such benefits.

ELECTION ACTS

Both the Ontario *Election Act* and the *Canada Elections Act* require that employers provide employees with at least three consecutive hours free from work to facilitate their voting in an election.

For example, if the polls are open from 8:00 a.m. – 7:00 p.m., and an employee's normal work day is 9:00 a.m. – 5:00 p.m., on election day the employer will either have to schedule the employee to come in at 11:00 a.m., or let the employee finish at 4:00 p.m.

Both Acts prohibit any deductions from an employee's pay as a result of the required time off being provided.

SMOKING IN THE WORKPLACE

Effective May 31, 2006, the *Smoke-Free Ontario Act* prohibits all smoking in any "enclosed workplace". This includes any place, building, structure or vehicle with a roof.

Employees may smoke on open patios so long as there is no food and beverage service on the patio.

The Act is enforced by a charge of a violation that is heard by a court. Maximum penalties of $100,000 for individuals and $300,000 for a corporation are set out in the Act.

Chapter 3

The Occupational
Health and Safety Act

GENERAL PROVISIONS

The *Occupational Health and Safety Act* (the "OHSA"):

(a) provides safety legislation for all employees in the province except farm workers who may be added by regulation;

(b) requires the establishment of joint health and safety committees, with employee representatives, selected by the employees equal in number to management representatives, for all workplaces with either 20 or more employees or where a regulation relating to a designated substance (or an order respecting a particular hazard) is in effect, except in the agricultural sector and at construction projects expected to last less than three months;

(c) provides for regular compulsory inspections of the workplace by joint health and safety committee members;

(d) gives employees the right to refuse to perform work that is likely to endanger, except in certain "high-risk" situations;

(e) requires posting of the OHSA and related explanatory material;

(f) requires that at least one employee be selected by the employees as a health and safety representative for workplaces and construction projects where over five persons are employed; and

(g) requires employers to prepare a health and safety program and implementation policy.

Application

The OHSA applies to virtually all blue-collar employment.

Regulations in the industrial, mining and construction field specify many of the requirements for such work. Specific, detailed regulations apply to employers that have in their workplace the following substances: acrylonitrile, arsenic, asbestos, benzene, coke oven emissions, ethylene oxcide, isocyanates, lead, mercury, silica and vinyl chloride.

Health and Safety Representatives and Committees

The OHSA specifies that joint health and safety committees shall be made up of at least two people; four if more than 50 employees are covered. At least half of the committee membership shall be non-managerial. The committee is to be co-chaired by an employee representative and a managerial representative.

Ministry of Labour officials consider it important that the committee have sufficient employee membership so that each distinct operation, and each operation involving "designated substances" (substances specifically dealt with by regulation) has its own representative.

The Minister of Labour has the authority to review and rule upon the adequacy of the committee when established. Such reviews usually only follow a complaint from an interested person. Upon receiving a complaint, an inspector from the Occupational Health and Safety Branch will meet with the employer to discuss the formation and operation of the committee. If the inspector is not satisfied with the committee he or she will propose changes to the employer first. If the inspector remains unsatisfied he or she can then prepare an Order directing the employer to proceed in a manner designed to ensure compliance with the OHSA.

The OHSA requires that:

(a) the committee keep and maintain minutes of its proceedings;
(b) the employee members of the committee choose one of their members to inspect the physical condition of the workplace at least once a month;
(c) the employee members choose one of their members to investigate cases where an employee is killed or critically injured;
(d) the committee meet at least once every three months;
(e) committee members' time in performing set out tasks and attending meetings be paid by the employer at appropriate, regular or premium rates;
(f) the committee may obtain from the employer information identifying potential or existing hazards;
(g) the committee may obtain from the employer information regarding safety testing, and committee members are to be present at the commencement of any such tests; and
(h) the committee, health and safety representative, an employee, employer or trade union may obtain from the Workplace Safety and Insurance Board an annual summary of data relating to the employer regarding work accident fatalities, lost work days, non-fatal cases that required

medical aid, incidence of occupational illnesses, and occupational injuries.

The joint health and safety committee provisions do not apply to construction projects expected to last less than three months. On such projects, if five or more employees are employed, the OHSA requires the employer to cause the employees to select at least one health and safety representative from among the employees on the project who do not exercise managerial functions.

The health and safety representatives have essentially the same responsibilities and authority as joint health and safety committee members outlined above, except that there is no requirement that regular meetings be held.

Safety Personnel Training

The OHSA provides for mandatory training of joint health and safety committee members and representatives. Once such persons have completed the required training, they will be "certified" representatives who will have the right to stop work under specified conditions.

Employers are required to ensure that an employee and a management member of each joint health and safety committee in the workplace are certified. Employers are required to pay for a training program, which is set by the Workplace Safety and Insurance Board.

The training requirement applies to provincially regulated workplaces with more than 20 employees. Construction projects lasting less than three months and which have fewer than 50 employees are exempt.

Right to Refuse Unsafe Work

The OHSA gives employees covered by it the right to refuse unsafe work.

Excluded from this provision are police, firefighters and certain correctional institutions and secure custody or temporary youth detention centres. Also excluded are employees in hospitals, sanatoriums, nursing homes, homes for the aged, psychiatric institutions, mental health centres, rehabilitation centres, certain residential group homes, ambulance services, first aid clinics or stations, a laboratory operated by the Crown or licensed under the *Laboratory and Specimen Collection Centre Licensing Act*, laundries, food services, power plants and technical facilities operated in conjunction with any of the foregoing.

An employee may refuse to work when the employee has reason to believe that:

(a) any equipment is likely to endanger him or her or another employee;

(b) the condition of the workplace is likely to endanger him or her;

(c) workplace violence is likely to endanger him or her; or

(d)   equipment or the workplace is in contravention of the OHSA or its
       regulations and is likely to endanger him or her or another employee.

When an employee refuses to perform work for one of these reasons he or
she is to immediately report to the supervisor who must investigate the
complaint and report to the employee and a joint health and safety committee
representative (if one exists).

If, following the investigation, the employee is instructed to proceed with the
work, he or she may still refuse. In this situation an inspector must be called to
investigate the matter in the presence of the employee, the committee representative
(if one exists) and someone representing the employer. During this time the
employee is to remain in a safe place at or near the work situation during his or
her regular working hours unless the employer, subject to the terms of a
collective agreement, assigns alternative work, or where other work cannot be
assigned, "gives other directions to the worker".

Pending the decision of the inspector, no other employee may be assigned the
disputed work unless he or she is told of the dispute and the reason for it.

If an employer "gives other directions" to an employee refusing the work in
question, it must be remembered that employer reprisals for the refusals are
prohibited. Keeping these preconditions in mind, it appears possible to temporarily
lay off employees in such circumstances. Reasonable alternative work must also
be unavailable before a lay-off takes place.

The OHSA prohibits employers from dismissing, disciplining, penalizing or
intimidating employees for conduct that is protected by the OHSA. Complaints
against employers in this respect may be processed under a collective agreement,
if there is one, or by the Ontario Labour Relations Board. The Board has held
that where a grievance procedure under an agreement is available, it should be
pursued before the employee goes either to arbitration under the agreement or to
the Board.

Required Postings

An employer covered by the OHSA must post and keep posted in a conspicuous
place:

(1)   the names and work locations of the joint health and safety committee
       members or representatives;
(2)   an annual summary from the Workers Safety and Insurance Board, if
       received;
(3)   a copy of the OHSA;
(4)   any explanatory material prepared by the Minister both in English and
       the majority language of the employees; and

(5)   the employer's Health and Safety Policy and Implementation Program, which must include a policy and program with respect to workplace violence and harassment.

The requirement to post explanatory material in the majority language of the employees should be read as being subject to its availability from the government. These materials can be obtained from the Ontario Government Book Store and are available on the Ministry of Labour website.

Workplace Violence and Harassment

While employers have had a long-standing obligation to keep employees safe in the workplace, effective June 15, 2010, amendments to the OHSA added specific definitions of "workplace violence" and "workplace harassment", along with specific employer obligations and duties regarding workplace violence and harassment.

All workplaces with more than five employees are required to prepare, implement and post a policy and program with respect to workplace violence and workplace harassment.

The policy and program must be reviewed as often as necessary and at least annually. Employers must provide training to employees regarding the workplace violence and harassment policy and program.

The amendments also require workplaces to conduct an assessment of workplace violence as often as necessary to determine the risks of workplace violence that may arise from the nature of the workplace, the type of work or the conditions of work. The employer must communicate the results of the assessment to the joint health and safety committee or representative, or, if none exist, to all of the employees. While the OHSA only requires an assessment of workplace violence, employers may want to consider also doing regular assessments of the risk of workplace harassment, given that harassment is often the first step towards a violent incident in the workplace.

An employer is required to take every precaution reasonable to protect employees if the employer becomes aware that domestic violence that would likely expose an employee to physical injury may occur in the workplace. Such precautions would include, at the least, that employers provide resources to an employee who is either exposed directly to domestic violence in the workplace (*e.g.*, his or her partner or ex-partner comes on to company property and threatens, attempts or engages in violence) or who is exposed to physical injury in the workplace as a result of another employee's domestic violence (*e.g.*, a co-employee's partner or ex-partner comes on to company property and threatens other employees). The Ministry of Labour has helpful resources on its website regarding domestic violence in the workplace, online: <http://www.labour.gov.on.ca/english/hs/pubs/wvps_guide/guide_6.php>.

Finally, employers are required to provide information, including personal information, related to a risk of workplace violence from a person with a history of violent behaviour if an employee is likely to be exposed to physical injury as a result of contact with that person in the course of employment. This will be particularly relevant in workplaces such as security facilities or nursing homes. While the employer is prohibited from disclosing no more personal information than is reasonably necessary to protect employees from physical injury, the challenge remains as to how to balance privacy and confidentiality rights with the positive employer duties introduced in the amendments to the OHSA.

Industrial Regulations

Since each industry will be affected by different safety regulations, the topics are too specific for general treatment here. Copies of industry-specific regulations are available online: <http://www.e-laws.gov.on.ca>.

The following are some of the regulations most commonly encountered in an industrial setting:

(a)   **Minimum age.** Employees in a factory must be at least 15 years old. In logging operations, 16 years old. Other employees must usually be at least 14 years old.

(b)   **Emergency lighting.** Emergency lighting for any area lit by artificial lighting is required. It must turn on automatically and be completely independent of the regular lighting service.

(c)   **Temperature.** The enclosed work space must normally be kept at a temperature "suitable for the type of work performed" and at least 18°C. Exceptions are made, for example, where perishable goods are being handled or where the need for open doors makes such heating impracticable.

(d)   **Washrooms.** Toilets must be provided in a fashion which gives the user reasonable privacy. Washbasins must have hot and cold water. If separate washrooms are provided they must be labelled as to gender. The washrooms must be reasonably equipped with supplies. The facilities required vary with the number of employees:

Employees	Toilets	Washbasins
1-9	1	1
10-24	2	2
25-49	3	3
50-74	4	4
75-100	5	5

Over 100 add 1 for every additional 30 employees or portion thereof.

(e) **Drinking water.** Drinking water must normally be made available from an upward jet fountain, or from a tap with a supply of cups on each floor of the premises and within 100 metres of every work area. Exceptions exist where hazardous substances are being handled.

(f) **Rest areas.** If 10 or more employees are employed, a reasonable private space must be provided with one or more cots or chairs (see also first aid room requirements in the section on the *Workplace Safety and Insurance Act* in Chapter 2).

(g) **Lunch rooms.** A suitable eating area must be provided if over 35 employees are employed.

Additional regulations cover safety considerations as diverse as confined spaces, diving operations, offshore oil and gas operations, guard rails, air venting, machinery safety devices, window cleaning and needle safety.

Enforcement

As noted under "Right to Refuse Unsafe Work" above, the OHSA is primarily enforced by inspectors employed by the Ministry of Labour.

Acting on their own initiative or as a result of an informal call or a required report, these inspectors have extensive rights, including the right to enter and inspect the workplace. Inspectors may make orders requiring compliance with the OHSA and Regulations. Once an inspector visits a workplace and makes an order, that order is standard. The most serious orders require work to be stopped in general or on a specific task until it is brought into compliance. Orders issued by inspectors may be appealed to the Ontario Labour Relations Board.

Inspectors can also issue "tickets" that carry specified fines in the hundreds of dollars each.

The Ministry can also charge individuals and corporations with an offence under the OHSA. Individuals may be fined up to $25,000 and imprisoned for up to 12 months. Corporations may be fined up to $500,000 per offence. In addition, the Government of Ontario has in place a Victim's Surcharge on all fines under the *Provincial Offences Act*. Such charges are determined by a court.

Criminal charges can also be brought against individuals and corporations, including supervisors and managers, who fail to properly ensure workplace safety or who act in a manner that causes unsafe conditions. Officers and Directors are responsible under the *Criminal Code* to ensure that reasonable steps are taken in the workplace to ensure safe working conditions.

WORKPLACE HAZARDOUS MATERIALS SYSTEMS

Introduction

The Workplace Hazardous Materials Information System ("WHMIS") is a national system which applies to all industries and all workplaces in Canada. Commonly referred to as Canada's first "right to know" legislation, it was designed to provide employees and employers with essential information about the usage, handling and storage of hazardous materials in the workplace.

Although the WHMIS is fundamentally an occupational health and safety issue and therefore generally a matter which falls within the constitutional jurisdiction of the provinces, a consensus was obtained for a pan-Canadian approach based upon core federal legislation and regulations. The rationale for this approach was a desire to ensure a uniform level of protection to all Canadian employees working with or in proximity to hazardous materials while at the same time avoiding the excessive costs and confusion which could result from the establishment of 13 separate provincial, federal and territorial systems.

Essential Elements of the WHMIS System

The WHMIS system is comprised of five principal features. These are:

(a) criteria for the identification and classification of hazardous materials;
(b) a cautionary labelling system for containers of hazardous materials;
(c) standards requiring the disclosure of information on documents called Material Safety Data Sheets;
(d) employee training and education requirements; and
(e) a procedure for ruling on supplier and manufacturer trade secrets and proprietary information claims.

Legislative Framework

The core federal legislation, which sets forth the details of the WHMIS system, is the amended *Hazardous Products Act* (the "HPA") and in particular, Part II of the HPA dealing with "controlled products". The principal regulatory provisions are the *Controlled Products Regulations*. This legislation is administered by Health Canada.

The second piece of relevant federal legislation is the *Hazardous Materials Information Review Act*. The core of WHMIS is to share information with stakeholders and regulators about the hazardous nature of materials in the workplace. Where this interest conflicts with a business's interest to retain trade secrets, the *Hazardous Materials Information Review Act* and its regulations has created a system that allows companies to make proprietary information claims to the Hazardous Materials Information Review Commission for an exemption from the HPA.

Most provincial governments have passed complementary occupational health and safety legislation authorizing the adoption of the WHMIS scheme in their jurisdiction. In Ontario, the Ministry of Labour has passed the WHMIS regulation under the *Occupational Health and Safety Act*.

Ontario has a number of additional regulations under the *Occupational Health and Safety Act* which impose employer obligations regarding hazardous materials and specific high risk industries. For example, effective July 15, 2010, Ontario consolidated 11 of its 12 regulations regarding hazardous chemical agents into one *Designated Substances Regulation* that requires specific assessments and employee training.

Identification and Classification of Controlled Products

Under the WHMIS, suppliers of potentially hazardous products (which means any person who is a manufacturer, processor or packager of a controlled product or a person who, in the course of business, imports or sells such products) are required to evaluate their products on the basis of the hazard criteria set forth in the federal *Controlled Products Regulations*. If a product meets the hazard criteria then it is a "controlled product" and must be classified according to the classification system set forth in the regulations.

Hazard Criteria Classes
Class A — Compressed Gas
Class B — Flammable and Combustible Material
    Division 1: Flammable Gases
    Division 2: Flammable Liquids
    Division 3: Combustible Liquids
    Division 4: Flammable Solids
    Division 5: Flammable Aerosols
    Division 6: Reactive Flammable Materials
Class C — Oxidizing Material
Class D — Poisonous and Infectious Material
    Division 1: Materials causing immediate and serious toxic effects
        Subdivision A: Very toxic materials
        Subdivision B: Toxic material
    Division 2: Materials causing other toxic effects
        Subdivision A: Very toxic materials
        Subdivision B: Toxic material
    Division 3: Biohazardous infectious material
Class E — Corrosive Material
Class F — Dangerously Reactive Material

Determining the Classification

For the purposes of establishing that a product, material or substance is included in one of the above-noted classes, a supplier shall generally use either:

(a)   results from testing that the supplier itself has carried out with respect to the product, material or substance in accordance with the relevant test procedures set forth in the regulations; or

(b)   an evaluation and scientific judgment based on test results with respect to the product, material or substance. In the case of potentially poisonous and infectious materials, the supplier may rely upon detailed toxicological information available from numerous well-known scientific sources.

Ingredient Disclosure

Where a product meets the hazard criteria and is classified under the WHMIS system, the supplier may be obliged to disclose, on Material Safety Data Sheets (see below) and otherwise, information concerning certain of the ingredients of the controlled product.

Such disclosure is required if any one of the following four conditions are met:

(a)   an ingredient of the product is itself identified as being hazardous under the WHMIS criteria set forth above;

(b)   an ingredient of the product is included on the Ingredient Disclosure List which is set forth as a regulation under the *Hazardous Products Act*, at a concentration level equal to or greater than the cut-off concentration level specified for that ingredient on the List;

(c)   the supplier has reasonable grounds to believe, based on its own testing or other knowledge of the material, that the ingredient may be harmful; or

(d)   the toxicological properties of the ingredient are not known to the supplier.

EXEMPTIONS

Certain kinds of products are specifically exempted from the WHMIS system and a supplier should initially determine whether or not any of the exemptions are applicable to its product. These exemptions relate to the following areas:

(a)   explosives within the meaning of the *Explosives Act*;

(b)   cosmetics, devices, drugs or food within the meaning of the *Food and Drugs Act*;

(c)   control products within the meaning of the *Pest Control Products Act*;

(d)   prescribed substances within the meaning of the *Nuclear Safety and Control Act*;

(e)   hazardous waste;

(f)   consumer products within the meaning of Part II of the *Hazardous Products Act*;

(g)   wood or products made of wood;

(h)   tobacco or products made of tobacco; or

(i)   manufactured articles within the meaning of the *Hazardous Products Act*.

Controlled Product Labelling and Warning Symbols

SUPPLIER LABELS

The HPA prohibits the sale or importation of a controlled product intended for use in a workplace unless the supplier provides a Material Safety Data Sheet and the required labelling in compliance with the HPA as well as the regulations.

Products which fall within the WHMIS system must contain documents called "supplier labels". These labels must satisfy the following five major requirements:

(a)   the label must be in both official languages;

(b)   information displayed on the label must be contained within a distinctive WHMIS border as depicted in Schedule III of the *Controlled Products Regulations*;

(c)   the colour of the label must contrast with the background of the container and must not create confusion with any other warning label or safety mark;

(d)   the label must be clearly and prominently displayed on the container; and

(e)   the label must be legible and durable enough to remain attached to the container under normal use.

The *Controlled Products Regulations* set forth the following minimum informational requirements with respect to supplier labels:

(a)   a "product identifier". This may be in the form of a chemical or trade name, code name or code number, generic name or common name; however it should be the name under which the material is sold. The product identifier on the label of the controlled product must match the product identifier on the Material Safety Data Sheet;

(b)   a "supplier identifier" (the name and business address of the supplier);

(c)   a "hazard symbol" (the standard pictograms specified for each class and division as set forth in Schedule II of the *Controlled Products Regulations*);
(d)   reference to the Material Safety Data Sheet;
(e)   appropriate risk phrases to describe the nature of the hazard, using appropriate words to describe the possible consequences of misuse of the product;
(f)   precautionary measures to be taken under conditions of normal use and possible emergency;
(g)   appropriate first aid measures in case of emergency;
(h)   where the supplier has made a request for exemption from disclosure of information under the *Hazardous Materials Information Review Act*, the label shall set out information relating to the date of the claim for exemption and the registration number of the claim.

Certain exemptions apply to containers to be used in laboratories and containers sold/imported which are 100 millilitres or less in volume.

So long as the controlled product remains in the container in which it was received from the supplier, the employer must ensure that the supplier label is not removed, defaced or modified in any way. Where the supplier label becomes illegible or is removed, the employer must replace the label with either a supplier label or a "workplace label" (see below under "Workplace Labels").

Where a multi-container shipment is received by an employer in circumstances where the individual containers have not been labelled by the supplier, the employer must affix to each container a label that meets the requirements of the *Controlled Products Regulations*.

BULK SHIPMENTS

In cases of bulk shipments, the employer must ensure that an appropriate supplier label or a workplace label is affixed, in accordance with the *Controlled Products Regulations*.

WHERE EMPLOYER PRODUCES CONTROLLED PRODUCT IN THE WORKPLACE

Where an employer produces a controlled product in the workplace, the employer must ensure that the controlled product or its container is labelled with a workplace label.

WORKPLACE LABELS

Workplace labelling requirements for controlled products are governed by provincial Occupational Health and Safety Regulations. Employers must ensure that containers of controlled products are properly labelled with a supplier label when they enter the workplace.

Workplace labels must satisfy the following content requirements:

(i) the label must provide a proper product identifier;

(ii) the label must provide information concerning the safe handling of the controlled product;

(iii) the label must contain a statement indicating that a Material Safety Data Sheet is available for the controlled product; and

(iv) the format of the workplace label is left to the discretion of the employer; however, the employer may wish to use a format similar to the supplier label for the purposes of recognition by employees.

PRODUCTS REQUIRING WORKPLACE LABELS

Workplace labelling requirements for controlled products are governed by provincial Occupational Health and Safety Regulations. Employers must ensure that containers of controlled products are properly labelled with a supplier label when they enter the workplace.

Where a controlled product is contained in a piping system, a reaction vessel,[1] a tank car or any similar conveyance system, the employer must ensure the safe use, storage and handling of the controlled product through labelling and the use of placards providing information similar to that provided on a workplace label.

SPECIAL LABELLING PROVISIONS

Special labelling requirements are established for laboratory samples to be used in a workplace, as well as for bulk shipments of controlled products.

Where a controlled product is shipped in circumstances where an outer container is labelled in accordance with the *Transportation of Dangerous Goods Regulations*, or where the label on an inner container is visible and legible under normal circumstances, no other label is required by the *Controlled Products Regulations*.

Material Safety Data Sheets

A supplier selling or importing a controlled product must provide a Material Safety Data Sheet for each controlled product on or before the first shipment to the purchaser.

---

[1] A holding tank in which a chemical reaction occurs, thereby producing a new chemical substance.

The following is a list of requirements applicable to Material Safety Data Sheets:

(a) the supplier must provide the Material Safety Data Sheet in either/or both official languages depending upon the preference of the purchaser. Where information is provided in both languages this may be accomplished through two separate Material Safety Data Sheets or on a single sheet at the discretion of the supplier;

(b) in Ontario, employers are required by the *Occupational Health and Safety Act* to make available Material Safety Data Sheets in English, French and the language of the majority of the employees in the workplace;

(c) Material Safety Data Sheets expire three years after the date of publication and must be routinely reviewed and updated by suppliers whenever changes in the data or information available with respect to the product or its ingredients become available;

(d) the format of the Material Safety Data Sheet is left to the discretion of the supplier.

Minimum informational requirements are set forth in the legislation with respect to Material Safety Data Sheets. These requirements are summarized as follows:

(1) hazardous ingredients (including chemical identity and concentration level);

(2) preparation information (*i.e.*, person, group or department who prepared the Material Safety Data Sheet, and the date the sheet was prepared);

(3) product information (including product identifier, supplier identifier and address, manufacturer's name and address, and product use);

(4) physical data relating to the properties of the controlled product;

(5) fire or explosion hazard information (if applicable);

(6) reactivity data (if applicable);

(7) toxicological properties (if applicable);

(8) preventive measures (including personal protective equipment, engineering controls, emergency procedures, waste disposal, handling procedures, proper storage requirements and shipping information);

(9) first aid measures;

(10) further information of which the supplier is aware;

(11) where a request for exemption from the requirement to disclose information has been made under the *Hazardous Materials Information Review Act*, the Material Safety Data Sheet must include information concerning the date of the claim and the registration number.

In addition, the following general obligations exist with respect to Material Safety Data Sheets:

(a) they must be readily available at the work site to employees who may be exposed to the controlled product;

(b) they must be made available to the joint health and safety committee or to a health and safety representative;

(c) training must be provided to employees and members of the joint health and safety committee with respect to measures to be taken to access all Material Safety Data Sheets;

(d) copies of unexpired Material Safety Data Sheets must also be made available to the following officials:

- the local Medical Officer of Health;
- the local Fire Department; and
- a Director of the Ministry of Labour.

Where an employer produces a controlled product in a workplace, the employer must provide a Material Safety Data Sheet for the product which complies with the requirements of the *Controlled Products Regulations*. Such a workplace Material Safety Data Sheet must be updated within 90 days after new hazard information becomes available to the employer, and at least every three years.

Training

Provincial legislation adopting the WHMIS scheme varies somewhat depending upon the province in which an employer operates. In a number of provinces, for example Manitoba and Ontario, the provincial scheme imposes additional obligations on employers.

In Ontario, the *Occupational Health and Safety Act* has included all hazardous biological and chemical agents as well as hazardous physical agents (which include such things as radiation, noise, heat and vibration) under the umbrella of the WHMIS system.

Substantial training obligations are set forth in the Ontario *Occupational Health and Safety Act* and its WHMIS regulation. Those training obligations apply to all aspects of work, not just to the use of hazardous materials. The *Occupational Health and Safety Act* imposes a general obligation on employers to provide "information, instruction and supervision" to employees to protect their health and safety. This section also requires employers to acquaint employees with hazards in the workplace and in the safe use, handling and storage of materials.

The *Occupational Health and Safety Act* further requires supervisors to advise employees of the existence of dangers to their health and safety, provide employees with written instruction with respect to proper procedures to be taken for their protection, and to take every precaution reasonable in the circumstances for the protection of employees.

The *Industrial Establishments Regulations* under the *Occupational Health and Safety Act* establish additional training obligations in respect of employees who may be exposed to certain types of chemical or physical agents which may endanger employee safety or health.

WORKPLACE WHMIS TRAINING OBLIGATIONS IN ONTARIO

In Ontario, employers must ensure that employees exposed or likely to be exposed to hazardous materials or hazardous physical agents receive and participate in adequate instruction and training. Such training must be developed by the employer in consultation with the joint health and safety committee or health and safety representative.

Employee training must be reviewed by the employer and the joint health and safety committee or health and safety representative at least annually, and more frequently if:

- the employer, on the advice of the joint health and safety committee or health and safety representative, determines that such reviews are necessary; or
- there is a change in circumstances that may affect the health or safety of an employee.

The *Occupational Health and Safety Act* requires employers to ensure that employees who either work with controlled products or in proximity to them are informed:

- about all hazard information received from suppliers in relation to such products; and
- any further hazard information of which the employer is aware or ought to be aware concerning such products and their use, storage and handling.

Although "supplier" is not defined in the Ontario WHMIS regulation, as indicated above, it is defined in the HPA as "a person who is a manufacturer, processor or packager of a controlled product, or a person who, in the course of business, imports or sells controlled products".

"Hazard information" is defined to mean information on the proper and safe use, storage and handling of a controlled product, including information relating to its toxicological properties.

The *Occupational Health and Safety Act* establishes similar obligations on employers where a controlled product is produced in a workplace, rather than received from a supplier.

The Ontario WHMIS regulation requires employers to ensure that employees who either work with controlled products, or in proximity to them, are properly instructed by means of an employee education program with respect to:

(a)   the content required on supplier and workplace labels;

(b)   the content required on Material Safety Data Sheets and the purpose and significance of such information;

(c)   procedures for the safe use, storage, handling and disposal of controlled products;

(d)   the safe use, storage, handling and disposal of controlled products contained or transferred in pipes and piping systems, certain types of vessels and rail cars, trucks and conveyor systems;

(e)   procedures to be followed in the event of fugitive emissions (which essentially means the escape of substances in various forms from emission control equipment or from the product itself); and

(f)   procedures to be followed in case of emergencies involving controlled products.

The Ontario WHMIS regulation also requires that employee education programs be developed and implemented for the employer's workplace and is related to any other training, instruction and prevention programs at the workplace. Employers must also ensure, so far as is reasonably practicable, that the employee education program results in an employee being able to apply the information as needed to protect his or her health and safety.

Enforcement of the WHMIS Scheme and Penalties for Violation

In most circumstances, the WHMIS scheme is enforced by provincial occupational health and safety inspectors under an agreement between the provincial and federal governments. Inspectors have been given additional search and seizure powers under the amendments including the following:

(a)   a right of access to the premises of suppliers and employers;

(b)   a right to examine and sample any product, material or substance believed to be a hazardous product and a right to examine anything used in the manufacture, preparation, processing, packaging, sale or storage of a hazardous material;

(c)   a right to examine and make copies of books or records;

(d)   a right of access to computer records and seizure of such records;

(e)   a right to seize any product, material or substance, or any labelling, advertising material or related matter in respect of which the HPA or regulations thereunder may have been contravened.

Detailed procedures and strict time limitations apply where the employer or supplier wishes to apply to the court to recover property seized by such inspectors.

The penalties applicable for violation of the provisions of the HPA relevant to the WHMIS scheme are as follows:

(a) on summary conviction a maximum fine of $100,000 and/or six months in jail or both; and

(b) on indictment a maximum fine of $1 million or imprisonment for a term of two years or both.

Any officer, director or agent of the corporation who directed, authorized, assented to, acquiesced in or participated in the commission of such an offence is a party to and guilty of the offence whether or not the corporation is prosecuted or convicted.

In Ontario, the maximum penalty for a person is a fine of $25,000 per offence or 12 months in jail and a fine of $500,000 per offence for a corporation. The courts are being asked to impose stiff penalties for failure to comply with the WHMIS scheme given the purpose of the legislation, the serious health and safety risks which employees face from hazardous materials in the workplace, and the significant health related claims under workers' compensation legislation in recent years.

Chapter 4

Pay Equity

The *Pay Equity Act* came into force on January 1, 1988. This legislation has had a major impact on compensation practices in the private and public sectors of this province.

In addition to the Act itself, the Pay Equity Commission has released the Pay Equity Implementation Series (originally known as the Guidelines) to assist parties in implementing pay equity.

APPLICABILITY

The *Pay Equity Act* requires every employer to establish and maintain compensation practices that provide for pay equity in every establishment of the employer. It applies to all public sector employers and all employers in the private sector who employ 10 or more employees.

If at any time an employer employs 10 or more employees, the Act applies, even though the employer may subsequently reduce the workforce to fewer than 10 employees.

The Act does not expressly define the term "employer". In an early decision, the Pay Equity Hearings Tribunal rejected the approach of the Ontario Labour Relations Board which generally focuses on a determination of who controls the key aspects of the employment relationship in determining the "employer". Instead, the Tribunal developed a fourfold test which sets out the indicia to assist in the determination of "employer" for the purposes of the Act as follows:

(1) Who has overall financial responsibility?
(2) Who has responsibility for compensation practices?
(3) What is the nature of the business, service or enterprise?
(4) What is most consistent with achieving the purpose of the *Pay Equity Act*?

Early decisions resulted in a very broad definition of "employer". A broader based employer expands possible job comparators among groups not otherwise comparable under the Act. For example, where a municipality was deemed to be the "employer" of both police and nurses, rather than the hospital employing the nurses and the Board of Commissioners of Police employing the police, job comparisons could then be made between police and nurses. Generally, the focus of the Tribunal has been on ultimate legal responsibility rather than practical day-to-day operational responsibility.

In a later decision, the Tribunal set out a scheme for applying the fourfold test where there is an existing collective bargaining relationship. The scheme is as follows:

(a)   identify the parties to the existing collective bargaining or employment relationship;

(b)   determine if the employer in that relationship controls the compensation practices and the value of the work;

(c)   apply the first two tests to elicit evidence upon which the Tribunal can determine who is the employer;

(d)   in the private sector, ask whether the work at issue is integral to the enterprise; and

(e)   if the answer is unclear, the fourth test may be used.

The early cases focused primarily on public sector employers. In later cases dealing with the private sector, the Tribunal considered a combination of the following factors:

- overall financial responsibility and control;
- responsibility for remuneration and compensation practices;
- direction and control over employees, including the assignment of work responsibilities and the setting of terms and conditions of employment;
- reasonable employee perceptions;
- the labour relations reality;
- the nature of the service, business or enterprise;
- control over determination as to the nature or scope of the service, business or enterprise; and
- consistency with the overall legislative purpose.

PURPOSE

The stated purpose of the Act is "to redress systemic gender discrimination in compensation for work performed by employees in female job classes".

To achieve this goal, every employer covered by the legislation is required to establish and maintain compensation practices that provide for pay equity in every establishment of the employer.

ACHIEVEMENT OF PAY EQUITY

Pay equity is achieved when the "job rate" for the female job class in issue is at least equal to the "job rate" for a male job class in the same establishment where the work performed in the two job classes is of equal or comparable value.

The "job rate" means the highest rate of compensation for a job class. "Compensation" means all payments and benefits paid to a person. In other words, the Act does not allow only wage adjustments. It requires an analysis of the value of benefits as well, although it contains no information on how this is to be done. The Pay Equity Commission provides 16 Implementation Service Guidelines to assist employers in achieving pay equity. Implementation Services Guideline #11 "Determining Job Rate" sets out some suggested options for doing so.

Essentially, the new legislation provides for equal pay for work of equal value, that is, where a female job is perceived to be of the same value to the employer as a male job, the two jobs must receive similar wages and benefits.

Where no "same value" comparison is available, comparisons may have to be made to jobs of lesser value but higher pay. See also "Proportional Value Comparisons" below.

COMPARISONS

To identify "systemic gender discrimination", comparisons are to be made between female job classes and male job classes in an establishment in terms of both compensation and value of the work performed.

Value of the work performed is measured by considering a composite of the skill, effort and responsibility normally required for the performance of the work and the conditions under which it is normally performed.

JOB CLASSES

A "job class" means those positions in an establishment that have similar duties and responsibilities and require similar qualifications, are filled by similar recruiting procedures and have the same compensation schedule, salary grade or range of salary rates.

A job class is "female" if 60 per cent or more of its members are female. A job class is "male" if 70 per cent or more of the members are male. However, in deciding whether a job class is female or male, the "historical incumbency" of the job class, "gender stereotypes of fields of work" and other criteria as prescribed by the regulations, must also be considered.

It is possible to have a job class consisting of only one position if it is unique in the establishment because its duties, responsibilities, qualifications, recruiting procedures or compensation schedule, salary grade or range of salary rates are not similar to those of any other position in the establishment. This will enable comparisons to be made between, for example, the sole female receptionist and a male job class in the employer's establishment.

As noted earlier, pay equity is achieved when the job rate for the female job class under review is at least equal to the job rate for a male job class in the same establishment, where the work performed in the two job classes is of equal or comparable value.

If there is no male job class of equal or comparable value with which to make a comparison, the workforce should be analyzed to determine whether there is a male job class which performs work of a lower value but has a higher job rate than the female class under scrutiny. If this is the case, the female job rate must be made equal to the job rate of that male job class.

If more than one comparison is possible, that is, there are a number of male classes performing work of equal value, then the job rate for the female class should be at least as great as the job rate for the equal value male job with the lowest job rate. In other words, the employer will only have to adjust the female wage rate to the level of the lowest job rate among the equal value male jobs.

Similarly, if there are a number of male job classes which, although receiving higher job rates than the female job class, are performing work of less value (and there is no equal value male job class), the comparison must be to that lower value male job class with the highest job rate.

GROUP OF JOBS

The Act provides that an employer may treat job classes that are arranged in a "group of jobs" as one female job class, if 60 per cent or more of the employees in the group are female. "Group of jobs" means a series of job classes that are organized in successive levels and bear a relationship to each other because of the nature of the work required to perform, the duties and the responsibilities of each job class in the series. An example would be Secretary 1, 2 and 3 or Technologist 1, 2 and 3.

The job rate for the group would be the job rate of the individual job class within the group that has the greatest number of employees.

PROPORTIONAL VALUE COMPARISONS

Proportional value comparisons allow for comparisons between job value and compensation paid to female job classes and job value and compensation paid to male comparator job classes.

The job-to-job comparison method, while recognized as appropriate where there are male job comparators available within the establishment, has been viewed as inappropriate in organizations that are all or predominantly female, or in organizations where there are female job classes for which there is no male comparator.

The proportional value method requires comparisons of the relative worth to an employer of female and male job classes where direct job-to-job comparisons are difficult to make.

The Act essentially requires implementation of proportional value in an establishment, in two circumstances:

- where job-to-job comparisons have not yet been made; or
- where there are some female job classes that do not have a male comparator, after job-to-job comparisons have been completed.

Plans that have been deemed approved under the Act will not need to be reopened if all female job classes have a male job class comparator. However, if any female job class in a deemed approved plan does not have a male job class comparator, the plan is required to be reopened and proportional value comparisons made for those female job classes without male job class comparators.

For pay equity plans that have not yet been deemed approved or required to be posted by the effective date of the amendments, proportional value comparisons will be available for use for the entire plan. However, a progressive approach may be used by applying job-to-job comparisons first and proportional value comparisons afterwards in order to capture all female job classes in the pay equity plan.

ESTABLISHMENT

Establishment is defined as all of the employees of an employer working in a "geographic division". Geographic division means a geographic area described under the *Territorial Division Act, 2002*.

In an establishment which is unionized, a pay equity plan is required for each bargaining unit and for that part of the establishment which is not in any bargaining unit. An employer and union may agree that the "establishment" includes two or more geographic divisions. In addition, in circumstances where central agreements are negotiated (such as province-wide bargaining in the construction trades, for example), the employers and union may agree that for the purposes of a pay equity plan, all of the employees constitute a single establishment and the employers shall be considered a single employer.

In non-unionized workforces, the employer may unilaterally decide that the "establishment" includes two or more geographic divisions.

PERMISSIBLE DIFFERENCES IN COMPENSATION

Differences in compensation between a female and male job class are permitted if the employer is able to show the difference is the result of the following:

(a)   a formal seniority system that does not discriminate on the basis of gender;

(b)   a temporary employee training or development assignment that is equally available to male and female employees and that leads to career advancement for those involved;

(c)   a merit compensation plan that is based on formal performance ratings, does not discriminate on the basis of gender, and has been brought to the attention of the employees;

(d)   red-circling, where the value of a position has been downgraded based on a "gender neutral re-evaluation process"; and

(e)   a skills shortage that is causing a temporary inflation in compensation because the employer is encountering difficulties in recruiting employees with the requisite skills for positions in the job class.

In addition, casual employees may be excluded in determining whether a job class is male or female and need not be included in compensation adjustments under a pay equity plan. However, any employee who works one-third of full-time hours, or performs work on a regular and continuing basis (even though not for one-third of full-time hours), or performs work on a seasonal basis, cannot be designated as a casual employee.

PAY EQUITY PLANS

Comparisons required under the Act for job classes inside a bargaining unit are initially to be made between classes in the bargaining unit. Similarly, job classes outside of a bargaining unit are to be compared to other non-bargaining unit job classes.

If there are no comparable male job classes within the same bargaining unit, a female job class within the unit can be compared to male job classes outside the bargaining unit in the same establishment.

In other words, if there are no male job classes within the bargaining unit of equal value, the employer must go outside of the bargaining unit to determine if there is a male job class of equal value in the establishment. If there is an equal value male job class, that class would form the basis of comparison. Note that the comparison, once it moves outside of the bargaining unit, is to be made in the "establishment". If the employer's establishment includes another bargaining unit, comparison could be to a job of equal value within that unit.

If there are no male job classes of equal value to compare to anywhere in the establishment then the range of possible comparables expands again. In such cases the employer is to look through the establishment for a male job class paid more but given a lower value. If such a class exists, it becomes the class to compare to. Both of these steps require a search outside the bargaining unit group and raise the need for valuation of possible outside comparable jobs on the same basis as unit jobs.

If this entire search fails to find a comparable job, then proportional value comparisons must be made.

The employer must negotiate in good faith with the union to agree upon:

(a) the gender-neutral comparison system; and
(b) a Pay Equity Plan for the bargaining unit.

Unionized Workplace

The Act contains no provisions that deal with the timing of pay equity negotiations. Consequently, employers and unions are free to decide to conduct such negotiations separately from the main collective bargaining negotiations. Although, from an employer's perspective, it would appear preferable to conduct negotiations simultaneously so that all wage adjustments, whether as a result of pay equity or other factors, would be considered at the same time. In actual practice, most employers and trade unions have conducted separate pay equity negotiations.

Employers and trade unions may agree (for the purposes of the Pay Equity Plan) that the "establishment" of the employer includes two or more geographic divisions and that a job class is male or female.

If the employer and trade union agree on a Pay Equity Plan, it will be deemed approved by the Pay Equity Commission. An approved Pay Equity Plan prevails over all relevant collective agreements and the compensation adjustments required by the Plan are deemed to be incorporated into the relevant collective agreements.

The Act specifically provides that the employer and union *cannot* bargain for or agree to compensation practices that do not provide for pay equity. If they cannot agree upon a gender-neutral comparison system or the Pay Equity Plan, they must notify the Commission of their failure to agree.

Once pay equity has been achieved in an establishment, differences in compensation between female and male job classes are permissible if the employer can show that they result from differences in bargaining strength. It is clear that many of the historical differences in wage rates which presently exist are the result of different bargaining strength between male and female dominated bargaining units. It would appear that this provision may lead, in the future, to a similar pattern of inconsistent wage rates. It seems somewhat incongruous that legislation designed to redress systemic wage discrimination would contain a provision which may allow future inequities to develop.

FAILURE TO AGREE

If the Pay Equity Commission is advised by an employer and/or trade union of their failure to reach an agreement on a Pay Equity Plan or receives notice of objection by employees in an unorganized workforce, a review officer shall investigate the matter.

The review officer will initially try to effect a settlement of the matter. If this is not possible, the review officer is empowered to decide all outstanding matters.

Decisions of the review officer can be appealed to the Pay Equity Hearings Tribunal which may confirm, vary or revoke orders of review officers.

ENFORCEMENT

Any employee, group of employees, union or employer may file a complaint with the Pay Equity Commission concerning contraventions of the Act.

In addition, any employee, group of employees or union may file a complaint alleging that:

(a)   a Pay Equity Plan is not being implemented according to its terms; or

(b)   because of changed circumstances in the establishment, the Plan is not appropriate for the female job class to which the employee belongs.

Such complaints will initially be dealt with by a review officer, who may attempt to settle the matter or issue orders to resolve it. Alternatively, the review officer may refer it to the Pay Equity Hearings Tribunal.

SALE OF A BUSINESS

The Act requires that the purchaser of a business make any compensation adjustments that were to be made under the vendor's pay equity plan to employees in positions maintained by the purchaser. The original compensation adjustment dates under the original plan would also apply to the purchaser.

Similar to the successor rights provisions in the *Labour Relations Act, 1995*, a "sale" includes "any manner of disposition", and a lease or transfer may fall within the definition of sale. These obligations apply even where only a part or parts of a business are sold.

If, as a result of the sale, either the seller's or the purchaser's plan becomes inappropriate, the seller or purchaser is required either to negotiate with the employee's bargaining agent with a view to agreeing on a new plan, or to prepare a new plan for employees not represented by a bargaining agent.

Chapter 5

Employment Contracts and Termination of Non-Union Employees

THE INDIVIDUAL CONTRACT OF EMPLOYMENT

All employment relationships are contractual. Collective agreements with trade unions are the most common form of written employer-employee contract. However, whether there is a union or not, whether the employee is a common labourer or the president of a large company, his or her employment is pursuant to a contract. The contract may be written or unwritten and if unwritten its terms may be clearly known to the employer and employee or just loosely understood by them. But there is always a contract.

If the contract is written, the employer and employee can agree to any provisions which are not in violation of the law. Most of the provisions of the *Employment Standards Act*, for example, are required minimums and cannot be taken away from an employee by the provisions of an employment contract. A contract does allow the parties, however, to deal with many matters that would not otherwise be part of their arrangement or that might be treated differently if a clear agreement between the parties did not exist. Since there are some results that the courts will impose upon the parties, in the absence of a contract providing otherwise, there are often advantages to ensuring that a clearly set out contract exists. Obviously, it is easiest to prove the existence of such a contract where the contract is in writing and is signed by both the employer and the employee.

The Advantages of a Written Contract

The advantage of a written contract is that it is clear evidence of the agreement which has been made between the parties. The advantage of a specific agreement depends on whether the parties wish to deal with items that are not otherwise dealt with by the law, or wish to deal with matters in a manner different than the normal legal rules. For example, employers may wish to avoid the assumption of constructive dismissal (discussed below) by specifically stating that they have the right to make changes in the employee's terms of employment without such changes being a termination of the relationship.

Employment contracts can deal with as many aspects of the relationship as the parties wish to specifically set out and, in special circumstances, can be detailed and lengthy documents. In most circumstances such contracts are actually quite short and deal with matters that have often proven to cause problems.

Termination Provisions

Canadian courts have said that every employment contract provides that an employee must be given reasonable notice of termination (or a payment in lieu of that notice) unless the termination is "for cause" (see the discussion below in "Termination of Non-Union Employees"). If the contract does not define "reasonable notice" it is not unusual for the courts to impose a one-year period and decisions have been made requiring as long as a two-year notice. Where the court is free to determine what reasonable notice is, it imposes a general guideline that reasonable notice should equal the period of time that it will likely take the employee to find a similar job.

In determining the period of notice required, courts consider the age, profession, experience, position, and length of service of the employee as well as any other factors relevant to the employee's ability to seek a similar job. If the notice period determined to be required by the courts has not been given, then the employer must pay termination pay in its place. The pay required is the amount the employee would have earned during the notice period, and includes benefits and regular bonuses; purely discretionary bonuses not a part of the employee's income may not be included.

However, the employee is under a duty to try to lessen his or her actual losses. Accordingly, the employee must seek other employment and any income received from that employment is deducted from the amount that the employer owes to the terminated employee.

Where the employment contract specifically sets out the required period of notice, the courts will accept the contractual provision unless it is completely unreasonable. A person who the courts may have found to be entitled to a 12- to 15-month notice may therefore be entitled to as little as a three-month notice pursuant to a written agreement. Not only does this provision reduce the cost to the employer of terminating an employee, it provides certainty to the parties and a remedy when problems occur in the employer-employee relationship by making termination a more affordable solution.

The notice period provided in a written contract must be a reasonable one and must at a minimum be equal to the notice of termination referred to in the *Employment Standards Act*. If the period is too short, a court may set it aside on the basis that it is not evidence of a true contract but rather of an unfair term imposed by the employer on an employee who either did not understand its meaning or had no choice but to accept it. Where the employee does have substantial bargaining power, even a very short notice period is likely to be accepted by the courts, so long as it at least meets the *Employment Standards Act* minimum.

Purpose of Employment

A written agreement allows the parties to specifically set out what the purpose of the employment is. This helps draw the attention of both parties to the question of exactly what it is they want the employment relationship to accomplish. It also helps to prepare the basis for a termination for cause should the employee not fulfil the employer's expectations of, and reasons for, the hiring of the employee.

Confidentiality

The agreement may set out that certain documents and other matters that may come to the attention of the employee are confidential to the employer. Manufacturers with secret manufacturing processes, technology companies with new technological inventions or employers who just want to protect their lists of sources, trade secrets and customers, may find such specific protection to be valuable. Similarly, sales companies may wish to protect their price structure information. As well as setting out what is confidential to the employer and what must remain with the company after the end of the employment relationship, the agreement may also specify what damages will result from breaching that confidentiality.

Non-Competition Provision

In many situations employers may wish to specify that employees are barred from taking actions that would compete with or injure the employer's business either during the term of employment or for a period of time following termination of employment. While it is often possible to include such a provision during the term of employment, it is difficult to bind the employee after employment is terminated.

The courts have imposed rules upon such clauses. These rules are designed essentially to ensure that the employee is free to seek and take up other employment. The court will allow such clauses where they are as limited as possible to accomplish the reasonable objective of the employer. In the case of a salesperson, therefore, the clause should probably be limited to the specific area serviced by the salesperson and, in time, to a period no greater than one year in duration, and if possible, to no more than three months. The more narrow the geographical and temporal scope, the more likely a court will uphold the provision. Even where the clause is specifically limited, the employer must still be prepared to show that it was necessary to protect its interest. It is easier to do this if, for example, the clause simply prohibits salespeople from soliciting orders from customers of their previous employer rather than prohibiting such salespeople from working in the same business at all.

Non-Solicitation Provision

Similar to the non-competition provisions discussed above, an employer may want to consider including a provision that limits the extent to which a former employee may solicit current employees to leave and join the former employee's new business. As with non-competition provisions, a non-solicitation provision should have as narrow a geographical and temporal scope as possible to increase the chance a court will uphold the provision. Canadian courts remain hesitant to enforce provisions that attempt to restrict labour mobility, unless there is a narrowly defined, legitimate and necessary business reason to do so.

A non-solicitation provision will be more valuable to an employer with critical employees that have very specialized knowledge. It is unlikely a court would uphold the provision for a general labourer.

Patents and Inventions

An employee, while engaged in work, may create an invention that will improve the work processes or the employer's product, and the employer may wish to guarantee that the invention will be its property. This can best be done with a provision in the agreement that specifically sets this out. Such a provision will also usually require the employee's full assistance in the patent application process.

Remuneration

The contract is, of course, a two-way document and the employee's remuneration and benefits are usually set out in the agreement. The wage clause can specify not only the current level of income, and how it is to be calculated, but also how it is to be reviewed and how often. Parties with complicated compensation schemes that include bonus, commission or stock option will greatly benefit from a clearly articulated understanding of remuneration.

This clause can also deal with such matters as life insurance, long-term disability insurance, vacations, holidays and other benefits that the employer provides to its employees.

TERMINATION OF NON-UNION EMPLOYEES

Unless special provisions exist in the employment contract, employees can be terminated either with notice (or a payment in lieu of the notice) or for cause (in which case no notice or payment is owed).

The contract may specifically deal with what constitutes cause. For example, a salesperson may be required to make a 10 per cent increase in sales annually. The contract may also set out what period of absence from employment for any reason, or for certain reasons, constitutes cause for termination. In most cases, however, general rules as to what constitutes cause will be applied.

The following are common grounds for termination with cause:

(a) dishonesty (usually sufficient cause);

(b) intoxication (will depend on the circumstances and the effect of the intoxication upon job performance; the *Human Rights Code* may provide protection if the employee has a proven addiction to alcohol or drugs);

(c) illness (temporary illness does not apply, but it does constitute cause if it leads to so much absence that the employee is not fulfilling his or her obligations; if the illness amounts to a disability, the employer has a duty to accommodate the employee's disability up to undue hardship);

(d) insolence (can be cause for termination, but generally must be fairly serious or extreme);

(e) incompetence (one of the toughest and yet most common reasons given as cause for termination; if incompetence is to be proven, the employer must be prepared to show what level of competence was expected, that this level of competence was known to the employee as being expected, and that it was not met); and

(f) conflict of interest (usually sufficient cause for termination).

The employer's inability to continue the employment for economic reasons is not cause for termination without notice, nor is the employer's change in methods of production or operations sufficient cause. In such cases, the employee will be entitled to notice of the termination or pay in lieu of notice.

It is important to note that reasons that might otherwise be sufficient cause will cease to be so if the employee's conduct has been condoned by the employer. An employer cannot therefore suddenly terminate an employee for insolence or absenteeism where that level of insolence or absenteeism has been tolerated many times in the past. An employer who has in the past condoned certain employee actions, but who does not wish to continue to condone them, must inform the employee of this change in advance. Condonation is a problem particularly where an employer wishes to discharge an employee for incompetence. In incompetence cases, the employer will usually have been found to have condoned the level of performance that the employee has been delivering. For example, where an employee has been doing the same job for several years at the same level of performance, or where an employee has been given raises, promotions or positive/neutral performance reviews, it will be most difficult for the employer to allege incompetence as the court will say the employer has condoned the employee's performance.

In the past, it was not unusual for a terminated employee to take whatever the employer offered and find another job. Today, more and more employees discharged either for cause, or with what they believe to be too short a notice period or too little severance pay, are seeking legal advice and threatening to sue their employers. A large portion of these cases are settled with the employer making an additional payment rather than risk the expense of losing a lawsuit. The amounts of these settlements are kept down by the employee's similar desire not to risk losing a suit or being known as someone who sued a former employer when going out on the job market to seek new employment. Employers must, therefore, carefully prepare their strategy in a termination situation before communicating their decision to the employee. In some cases, especially where the termination of executives is motivated by economic circumstances, companies engage the services of specialized management consultants or career coaches to assist in the termination and aid the employee in finding a new job. Not only does this discharge some of the company's moral responsibility to the employee, it also lessens any possible claim for damages as a result of the dismissal.

Employees may also claim that their termination violated the *Human Rights Code* and seek extra damages or special orders from the court as well. While courts continue to refuse to reinstate non-unionized employees, courts may award additional damages for breach of the Code.

Employers who are considering terminating an employee for cause should be aware that it has been very difficult to prove the existence of cause in court. This is especially true where, as is usually the case, there is no specific written contract that the employee is failing to live up to.

If incompetence or poor performance is the reason for the termination, the employer should be prepared to show that the employee was made aware of the standard expected, was warned about the consequence of failing to meet the expected standard, and was given ample opportunity to improve. In order to prove these warnings in court they should be in writing and receipt should be acknowledged by the employee.

A method used by some employers is to meet with the employee to discuss the failure to meet expectations and to place the employee on a mutually agreed upon performance improvement plan. Such a plan would specify the clear objectives the employee must meet, should have a timeline of at least one to three months for the employee to improve, and should be signed by both the employee and employer. This provides both parties with a document that demonstrates good faith attempts to improve the employee's performance, while providing the employer with a tool to terminate an employee should the performance not improve, despite such efforts.

If the termination is going to be for cause, the employer should start preparing for the potential legal suit even before the employee is terminated. It is important that the employer prepare its evidence of the employee's failures as early as possible in the process. For example, supervisors and fellow employees with complaints about the employee should be told to record their complaints in writing. Documents regarding the employee's performance should be gathered, reviewed and safely stored. All relevant emails and electronic transmissions and copies of performance reviews should be preserved. If the reason for termination has anything to do with Internet or other technological activity, all such data should be immediately saved.

The advice of legal counsel, who may eventually be called on to defend the case, should be sought before the termination. If the employer waits until the employee's lawyer writes the company threatening a lawsuit before it seeks legal advice, it will be too late to take many of the steps that can best assist its defence.

Constructive Dismissal

There are actions that employers can take that may be considered termination by a court even though the employer did not view them that way. These actions are called "deemed terminations" or more commonly, "constructive dismissals".

For an employee to make a claim of constructive dismissal, the employee must prove to the court that the employer behaved in such a manner so as to force the employee to consider such behaviour as indirectly terminating the employee. In such cases, the employee must generally resign and then sue the employer, a large risk that many employees hesitate to take.

If an employee does successfully prove a claim of constructive dismissal, he or she will be entitled to the usual notice (or pay in lieu of notice).

The following are some of the more common examples of behaviour that could amount to a constructive dismissal.

Changes in Location

The most common form of constructive dismissal is requiring an employee to move to another location to continue employment. Unless the contract of employment specifically allows the employer to transfer the employee, such a forced move will usually be considered a termination if the employee wishes to treat it that way.

A general manager hired to run a plant in Toronto may therefore consider himself or herself terminated if the employer tells the manager to move to

Edmonton to run its plant there. The fact that the employer will pay all expenses involved, or even that the move is a promotion, does not necessarily matter.

A written contract may, of course, specifically allow the company to make such transfers and companies that operate in such a manner should include an appropriate clause. Where no written or specific contract exists it may be possible to show that the circumstances are such that the unwritten contract allowed for such moves. This might be the case with salespeople who knew that the company changed assignments regularly, or with employees of large nation-wide employers who knew transfers were a common occurrence when they accepted the job.

If the employee can consider a requirement to move to be termination, then the employee is entitled to reasonable notice as in any other non-cause discharge.

Change in Compensation

Significant changes in salary or benefits may be treated by an employee as a termination. For example, it may amount to constructive dismissal if an employer unilaterally restructures a bonus or commission plan and makes it impossible for an employee to achieve previous compensation levels. Alternatively, the employee may elect not to treat him or herself as terminated and sue the employer to recover the lost wages over a reasonable period.

Changes in Responsibilities

A change in duties or responsibilities may be treated by an employee as a termination. So too may a change in the employee's reporting arrangement, especially if it can be seen as a demotion. The perspective of the employee will be considered important to whether the change is seen as a demotion. These changes may be considered a constructive dismissal even though there is no reduction in salary or benefits.

This legal view of such changes can cause problems for both a successful and expanding company and a company that has to tighten its belt. In both cases, employees are likely to find their responsibilities and their reporting positions changing. For example, if a company decides to restructure and limit its former Vice President of Marketing and Sales to just sales in order to hire a new marketing executive, the Vice President may be able to claim that the change constitutes a termination of employment.

More commonly, companies may seek to reassign and reduce the duties of persons whose performance is marginal or inadequate by its current standards. Unlike the senior executive being relieved of a burdensome task, who may welcome the change, an employee who is being demoted is much more likely to decide to treat the company's action as termination and seek pay in lieu of notice.

In either case, including a provision in the employment contract that permits management changes to meet the business needs of the organization may assist with lowering the risk of a successful constructive dismissal claim.

The law of constructive dismissal is set out in court decisions and this law continues to develop over time. Precise guidelines cannot be set out and employers must be alert to the problems that can develop if employees do not like the changes that are required of them.

Resignations

When an employer invites an employee to "resign or be fired" the resultant resignation will be considered a termination of employment.

In any resignation situation the employer's actions may be closely reviewed by a court to see if the employer in fact triggered the resignation. If the court finds the employer caused the resignation, it will consider it to be a termination. If the employee resigns rather than accepting a change in responsibilities or a relocation, the resignation will probably be considered a constructive dismissal.

In all cases of resignation, courts require a clear and unambiguous intention to resign. Any equivocal statements or behaviour that suggest dissatisfaction with the job but not necessarily a resignation will be questioned by the court. For example, if an employee walks out after a heated argument with his or her supervisor, but does not necessarily state that he or she resigned, the employer will want to obtain clear confirmation afterwards of the employee's intentions.

Where an employee does in fact resign freely, the employer should get the resignation in writing to help avoid any later disputes.

Chapter 6

The Arrival of a Trade Union

THE NON-UNION ENVIRONMENT

In today's workplace an employer with a workforce that could be unionized must recognize that it is government policy to ensure that all employees have the right to join a union. Furthermore, that policy, as it is expressed in the *Labour Relations Act, 1995*, guarantees trade unions the right to organize employees.

The law, discussed in detail later in this chapter, provides strong remedies for employees, and for trade unions, who feel that their right to organize and be organized has been interfered with by an employer.

Most employees are, however, normally reluctant to join a trade union. This natural hesitancy can be overridden by the irritation caused by bad employee relations.

Four areas can be identified as contributing to good employee relations: communication; employment security and discipline; wages and benefits; and working conditions.

Communication

Communication is the first and most important area of concern. Without effective communication, improvements in the other areas will not have their full benefit. Good communication must come from both sides. Policies, procedures, changes in working conditions and general wage and benefit changes must be communicated to employees. At the same time, dissatisfaction over any issue, as well as positive suggestions for improving working conditions and productivity, must be communicated by the employees to the employer. Such a policy can be implemented through the use of committees, intranet communication boards or emails, suggestion boxes, meetings at various levels and by generally maintaining an open-door management policy.

Many an employer has been unionized because employees were upset about an issue that could have been rectified had the employer only known about it.

Employment Security and Discipline

Job security is always a major issue with employees, particularly in difficult economic times. Their security is threatened by the possibility of lay-offs as well as by management's unfettered right to discharge for disciplinary reasons. It is in this area of employment that unions offer the greatest advantage to employees. Almost every collective agreement in the province imposes restrictions on the employer's choice of whom to lay off when lay-offs are necessary. Their restrictions usually recognize, in various ways, employee seniority. Similarly, the collective agreement will restrict an employer's right to discharge an employee, usually requiring that such discharges only be for just cause.

In order to respond to these concerns employers should consider implementing, and making known, lay-off policies that respect employee seniority as much as possible. For example, a policy of "last in-first out" can be adopted subject to the company requiring employees with certain skills or abilities. Such a policy can be adopted on a company-wide or department-wide basis. Consideration should also be given to seniority when employees are being promoted or transferred. A policy of promoting the most senior applicant of those with relatively the same level of skill and ability should be considered. The adoption and implementation of such policies should be continually communicated in a transparent manner and should be well documented to assist management in defending any future decisions based on the lay-off and promotion/transfer policies.

In the area of discharge and discipline it is important to adopt policies that assure employees they will be fairly treated. A commitment to progressive discipline with warning slips as a first step and discharge as a last resort can be considered. In many circumstances, it is advisable to set up a review procedure for any discipline imposed by a first-line supervisor and to limit the number of people authorized to discharge an employee to a few persons within top management. Again, transparency regarding the process followed in discharge and discipline matters helps eliminate misunderstandings or suspicions of unfair treatment.

Wages and Benefits

The key to maintaining an acceptable level of wages and benefits is to ensure that the company is competitive both with other industries of the same type and with other employers in the immediate area. A survey of such employers once or twice a year can be undertaken to provide the necessary information.

There are a number of online resources available to employers to determine comparable wages in various industries. It should be kept in mind that, of course, employees also have access to such information, which may raise expectations when negotiating salaries.

Two useful resources include the federal government's website, Labour Market Information, online: <http://www.labourmarketinformation.ca> and the Ontario government's website for disclosure of public sector salaries above $100,000, online: <http://www.fin.gov.on.ca/en/publications/salarydisclosure/2010/>. Employers may want to communicate to employees the steps they take to ensure wages and benefits are competitive.

Working Conditions

Again, the first step to maintaining good working conditions is effective communication. Most studies surveying employee satisfaction rank feeling valued in the workplace higher than salary, so it is beneficial for employees to have a route for expressing their concerns to management. The second step is ensuring that once a concern has been made known to management, it is either corrected or the reasons for being unable to correct it are explained to the affected employees. Where an improvement is planned but will take some time to implement (such as the installation of air conditioning) this should be made known to employees. Where remedial action cannot be taken for some reason (such as it being too expensive) this also should be made known to employees.

RESPONDING TO AN APPLICATION FOR CERTIFICATION

The Labour Relations Board

Often the first time an employer knows that its employees have decided to join a trade union is when it receives notice of an application for certification from the Ontario Labour Relations Board (the "Board").

The Board is an independent government body, much like a court. The major difference between the Board and a court is that the Board's authority is limited to labour law matters and its membership is made up of individuals expert in that area. The Board is tripartite, which means that it is composed of representatives of management, labour and neutrals. The neutrals include a chairperson and a number of vice-chairs. Cases before the Board are often heard by three members — one member representing each side and one of the neutrals, either the chair or a vice-chair.

The Board conducts its hearings in Toronto, in hearing rooms located at 505 University Avenue and occasionally in major cities around Ontario if the people involved come from, or from near, one of those other centres. The hearings are increasingly legalistic and the parties are more often represented by either a lawyer or an experienced union representative. Unrepresented parties should prepare by reviewing the Board's Forms, Information Bulletins and Rules of Procedure, all of which are available on the Board's website, online: <http://www.olrb.gov.on.ca>.

The Board issues approximately 6,500 decisions per year. Prior decisions of the Board are not absolutely binding in any case, but the Board looks to them for guidance. In many areas, 60 years of decisions have resulted in policies being set down that are very inflexible, and it is important for parties to understand the expectations of both the Board and the other parties. Board decisions are publicly available online at <http://www.canlii.org/en/on/onlrb/index.html>. By the end of 2010, the online decisions will date back to 1977, with only limited key decisions prior to that. Any member of the public can visit the Ontario Workplace Tribunals Library at 505 University Avenue in Toronto for hard copies of all Board decisions (<http://www.owtlibrary.on.ca>).

The Board employs a staff of civil servants who process the documents and a field staff of labour relations officers who perform various duties designed to expedite and to settle matters coming before the Board.

The Board's authority extends over most of the private sector in Ontario. It excludes federally regulated enterprises such as banks, inter-provincial transportation and the communications industry. It also excludes employees of the federal and provincial governments. Firefighters, police officers and teachers are covered by other legislation. Employees of municipal governments, however, do fall under the Board's jurisdiction.

The Board's major job is to process applications for the following:

- certification for bargaining rights (approximately 1,000 per year);
- contraventions of the *Labour Relations Act, 1995* (approximately 700 per year); and
- construction industry grievances (which must go before the Board rather than a private arbitrator, at the rate of approximately 1,000 per year).

In most situations, certification, or the right of a trade union to represent employees, has come about as a result of a Board Certificate (discussed below).

Although rarely used, another way in which a union may be certified is when an employer's behaviour is so egregious that the employees' true wishes cannot be ascertained through a representation vote. In such a case, the Board has the power to order certification of the union as a remedy (remedial certifications were removed from the Board's powers in 1995 but reinstated in 2005).

Finally, it is also possible in Ontario for an employer to grant voluntary recognition to a trade union. Voluntary recognition is rare outside the construction industry. In the construction industry it may be important for an employer to be considered unionized in order that it may bid for a specific job. As a result the employer voluntarily recognizes a union. During the first year of a voluntary recognition any employee can make an application to the Labour Board for a declaration that the trade union did not represent a majority of the employees at the time of the voluntary recognition. Apart from this one difference, a trade union's rights following a voluntary recognition are no different than following a Board Certificate.

Who Can Apply for Certification and When?

The provisions regarding certification in the Ontario *Labour Relations Act, 1995* start with the important provision that "a trade union may apply ... to the Board for certification as bargaining agent of the employees in the unit". The Act defines "a trade union" as "an organization of employees formed for purposes that include the regulation of relations between employees and employers".

There is no magic in the organization's name and many groups that are trade unions under the *Labour Relations Act, 1995* call themselves other things, such as "associations". The Board determines whether a group is a trade union the first time the group makes an application to the Board. The Board confirms that the members of the organization are employees, that it has a constitution which includes a clause that sets out as one of the organization's purposes the regulation of relations between employees and employers, and that it has officers who can carry out the organization's purposes. Once the Board has declared that an organization is a trade union, it issues the decision and the declaration is good for all subsequent cases unless challenged.

An application for certification can generally be made when there is no existing trade union that has the right to represent the employees. When there is a trade union already in existence, another trade union can apply only during certain limited times. These times include the last three months of any collective agreement or, where there is no collective agreement, any time after a year has gone by since the last agreement or since the current trade union was certified.

The Appropriate Bargaining Unit

On an application for certification one of the major jobs of the Board is to determine which employees should be included in the unit that the trade union will represent. This unit is called the "appropriate bargaining unit".

The Board's general approach is to include in the unit all those employees who share a community of interest. To this end, the Board will consider the nature of the work involved, the skills of the employees and the dependence or independence of the various work groups under consideration. The Board will also look at the history of collective bargaining in the particular industry and the employer's own organizational structure. In general, the Board prefers larger rather than smaller units and is against segmenting groups that could be together.

As a result of these policies, a typical manufacturing enterprise will be made up of two bargaining units. One unit will comprise all of the employees in the factory; the second unit will be made up of all the employees in the office. Part-time employees and summer students will probably be separated from full-time employees in a single bargaining unit unless the union and employer agree, although this once almost automatic separation is under review.

Certain groups of employees are excluded from the rights granted by the *Labour Relations Act, 1995*. These exclusions include persons employed in agriculture and horticulture. However, this exclusion has been held to be unconstitutional by the Supreme Court of Canada and as a result, the Ontario government enacted the *Agricultural Employees Protection Act, 2002*. While the *Agricultural Employees Protection Act, 2002* provides some protection for agricultural employee bargaining, certain labour groups have appealed the limited protections to the Supreme Court of Canada. At the time of writing, the matter is still under review by the Supreme Court and it remains to be seen the extent to which agricultural and horticultural employees can unionize in Ontario.

Also excluded from the collective bargaining rights in the *Labour Relations Act, 1995* are police, fire service employees and teachers, all of whom are covered by other laws granting special rights to union representation.

Special rules regarding the appropriate bargaining unit exist for employees exercising a particular craft, usually found in the construction industry. In the construction industry the appropriate bargaining unit is all employees who are engaged in one of the traditional crafts such as carpentry. General labourers also form one appropriate bargaining unit. A union can make an application for all employees of a construction employer to be included in one unit, but the *Labour Relations Act, 1995* gives applications for craft groups a special preference.

The appropriate bargaining unit must exclude those employees who are employed in a managerial capacity. In order to identify managerial employees, if there is a dispute, the Board applies a number of tests. These tests include determining the individual's control over the workforce, supervisory authority, right to make unreviewable decisions, and participation in the formulation of policy. For most situations, prior Board decisions provide a clear indication as to where the Board will draw the line. In the typical industrial setting, the Board usually draws the line at non-working foremen, who are excluded. Lead hands are usually included in the unit. The underlying concern behind this policy is to prevent a conflict of interest within the bargaining unit or within management.

Similarly, employees who are employed in a confidential capacity in matters relating to labour relations are excluded. For employees to be excluded under this rule they must have a regular involvement in the employer's labour relations. Simple access to confidential material will not be sufficient cause to exclude the employee.

Required Support for the Union

In order to be certified by the Board, a trade union in the industrial sector must win a representation vote of all employees in an appropriate bargaining unit. The Board will order a representation vote when the union asserts in an application for certification that 40 per cent or more employees of a proposed bargaining unit are members of the union. The usual method for unions to assert that employees are members of the union is to have them sign union membership cards. The employer may challenge this assertion if it can show facts that suggest the percentage is not 40 per cent such as employment records indicating a much higher number of total employees.

In the construction industry, the Board will accept union dues books as evidence of membership in place of membership cards. Further, if the membership evidence indicates support exceeding 55 per cent the Board may, and usually will, certify the union without a vote being held.

The Application Procedure

The process starts when the trade union delivers its application for certification to the employer and files a copy with the Board. Information Bulletins outlining the required Forms and documents are located on the Board's website, online: <http://www.olrb.gov.on.ca>. The Board will then fax or deliver a package to the employer. The package from the Board includes a notice to the employees which the employer is required to post on its premises in locations where it will come to the attention of the employees. The employer must return to the Board an enclosed form confirming that it has posted the notice to the employees.

Forms are also provided for the employer to respond to the union's application. As part of its response, the employer is required to provide the Board with lists of the employees employed at the time of application. The employer sets out its name and address and information concerning the number of employees in the bargaining unit on the reply form provided. The employer should describe the bargaining unit that it feels is appropriate for collective bargaining purposes. The employer may also inform the Board of any other relevant matters such as the presence of another trade union.

Within a day or two, the Board will review the union's application to determine whether it appears to have the required 40 per cent support and then order a vote. If the employer disputes the existence of such numerical support, it must do so quickly on the forms provided. A labour relations officer will contact the employer to discuss vote procedure.

A vote will be held five working days after the Board receives the union's application unless the Board orders otherwise. On the day of the vote, if there is any dispute about whether employees should be in the bargaining unit, the labour relations officer conducting the vote will segregate and not count those employees' votes. Later, the Board will decide whether the employees whose ballots were segregated had the right to vote. The actual vote may or may not be counted in the meantime, depending on many factors.

In most cases, the union will be certified without a hearing ever being held. The Board has found that the parties abandon most of their disputes about details once the result of the vote is known.

The union will be certified if more than 50 per cent of those voting, vote in favour of union representation.

THE FREEZE ON WORKING CONDITIONS

From the time that the employer receives notice from the Board that the union has applied for certification, its right to change the employees' working conditions is restricted by the *Labour Relations Act, 1995*. Section 86(2) of the Act says:

> Where a trade union has applied for certification and notice thereof from the Board has been received by the employer, the employer shall not, except with the consent of the trade union, alter the rates of wages or any other term or condition of employment or any right, privilege or duty of the employer or the employees …

This freeze continues until the Board turns down the union's application for certification, or, if the application is successful, until either a collective agreement is signed between the parties or the right to strike or lockout arises (the timing of the right to strike or lockout is discussed in Chapter 7 under "Strikes and Lockouts").

The policy behind the freeze on changing any employee working conditions upon the commencement of a certification drive is to ensure the employees' true wishes are ascertained, without the potential influence of employer promises such as new wage increases or improvements in working conditions.

The extent of the freeze has been a matter of much debate inside and among the various Labour Boards operating in Canada. In Ontario, the Board has held that the freeze simply requires that the employer continue in a "business as usual" manner. This approach allows an employer who had previously decided to install a new machine to proceed with its installation and to change working conditions accordingly. It also requires that an employer who had made an earlier announcement of an increase in wages proceed at the announced time with implementation of the increase. It probably prohibits, however, wage increases not previously announced or major changes in working conditions not previously planned and not consistent with an earlier history of changes.

The area is not an easy one and there are many problems which do not clearly fall into the frozen or not frozen categories.

A similar freeze on working conditions commences when a collective agreement expires and likewise continues until a strike or lockout is timely under the *Labour Relations Act, 1995*.

THE LABOUR BOARD HEARING

Board hearings look very much like court proceedings. There are often a number of cases to be dealt with in the same day and they are usually all scheduled for the same time with the result that people may be waiting until their turn is called by the Board. It is, however, very important that parties to Board proceedings arrive on time as the Board can, and will, proceed to decide the case in their absence.

In a certification application, the Board will hold a hearing if there are any issues in dispute that cannot be settled by the Board's staff. Since the applicant union will usually have been before the Board on previous occasions, the Board will simply announce that a prior determination about status has been made and that there is a note in the file to that effect.

The Board then proceeds to determine what the appropriate bargaining unit is. Outstanding issues such as whether a person is managerial or otherwise in or out of the unit are now dealt with. At the Board hearing, each of the parties has the right to produce evidence, to present witnesses, to question those witnesses presented by other parties or the Board, and to be represented by counsel if it wishes.

Labour relations officers will approach the parties to settle these matters even before the Board actually conducts its hearings. If the officer is successful and the parties have agreed on all outstanding matters, they do not have to appear at a formal Board hearing.

Where there are outstanding matters that require a longer hearing, the Board will still grant certification to the union on an interim basis if it is clear that, no matter how the outstanding issues are resolved, the union will have won the vote. For example, if the union has the support of 70 voters, and it is unclear whether there will be 100 or 105 total votes counted, the Board will grant interim certification because the union will have over 50 per cent support no matter what the final result is.

CONDUCT OF A CERTIFICATION VOTE

The vote is conducted by way of a secret ballot, presided over by a Board labour relations officer. Following the vote, the Board officer, in the presence of scrutineers appointed by both sides, will likely count the ballots and prepare a report to the Board setting out the results. The officer will usually count the ballots immediately even though certain employees have had their ballots separated in sealed envelopes pending a decision as to whether they had the right to vote. If the result of the vote is clear, then a decision regarding the separated ballots will probably never be made.

UNFAIR LABOUR PRACTICES

The *Labour Relations Act, 1995* contains a number of provisions designed to protect the employee's right to join a union, and the union's right to organize and represent employees, free from employer interference.

The *Labour Relations Act, 1995* prohibits employers and their representatives and agents from:

(a)   interfering in a union's organizing campaign;

(b)   firing a person, or refusing to employ a person, because of their support for, or membership in, a union;

(c)   restricting a person's right to join a union; and

(d)   intimidating, disciplining or in any way discriminating against a person because of their support for, or membership in, a union.

The *Labour Relations Act, 1995* also prohibits employer support of a trade union.

Complaints that an employer has violated these provisions are often made during a union organizing campaign. The most common complaint is that the employer has fired an employee because of the employee's support for the union.

Another common complaint made to the Board is that the employer has interfered in the organizing campaign. Such complaints often allege that the employer has threatened employees to not join the union, possibly in a speech or in a memo distributed to all employees.

While the *Labour Relations Act, 1995* specifically preserves the employer's right to free speech, the Board has repeatedly found that threats designed to stop employees from joining a union are prohibited by the Act. Such threats are often found to be in the form of a suggestion that the company might close down if a union is certified. In one case, the distribution of newspaper clippings by the employer that reported on plant shutdowns, lay-offs and long strikes after unionization, was held to violate the *Labour Relations Act, 1995*.

If a complaint is made to the Board that the employer has treated any individual in a way that violates the *Labour Relations Act, 1995*, then a special provision of the Act requires that the employer prove that the complaint is not true. Obviously, this is different than the usual situation where the person who complains of a violation must prove it. This reversal of the "burden of proof" requires that employers must be that much more careful about any actions they take once they know a union organizing campaign is underway.

Once a complaint is made to the Board, an officer of the Board is appointed to try and settle the case. In Ontario, the officer's only duty is to try and get a settlement. If unsuccessful, the officer does not include in the report to the Board what he or she has found out.

The officer will first contact the complaining party to get more details of the complaint and to discover whether he or she is willing to settle the matter. Then the officer will meet with the employer to learn its side of the story and see if a settlement is possible. Approximately 75 per cent of all complaints are settled by the officer at this stage. For example, employees who have been fired for union activity or support are usually reinstated by the employer when it learns of the provisions of the *Labour Relations Act, 1995*.

At the same time as the Board appoints an officer, it also sets a hearing date. This date is usually four to five weeks from the day the Board receives the complaint. By the time the employer learns of the hearing, however, there may be as little as three weeks left. The Board will usually grant adjournments only if both sides agree, so the hearing usually proceeds on the scheduled date unless settled. The Board will not usually accept the unavailability of the employer, its lawyer, or any other person as a reason for an adjournment.

The Board can make a wide variety of orders if it finds an employer has violated the *Labour Relations Act, 1995*. An employer may be, among other things, told to:

(a) rehire people with full back pay;

(b) post a notice that it had violated the *Labour Relations Act, 1995*;

(c) allow the union to meet with employees on company time;

(d) provide a bulletin board for the union's use; and

(e) pay the union's organizing costs.

In addition, if the Board finds that the employer's improper conduct made the results of a representation vote unreliable, the Board may order the vote to be reheld. In certain circumstances considered very serious by the Board, the Board may certify the union without holding a vote or despite the result of a vote.

If the Board finds that any of its orders are not being obeyed, it may file its decision with the Ontario Court of Justice whereupon it becomes a decision of the court. Should the order still not be obeyed then contempt of court proceedings can follow.

Board decisions are not normally subject to appeal to the courts. However, in very limited circumstances, if the Board makes a fundamental legal error its decision can be reviewed by a court.

Chapter 7

The Relationship With a Union

POST CERTIFICATION EVENTS

Once the Ontario Labour Relations Board (the "Board") has certified the union as the representative of a group of employees, the employer is required to deal exclusively with the union regarding the terms and conditions of employment of those employees. An employer can no longer negotiate directly with individual employees.

Following certification, the union will send the employer a notice to bargain for a collective agreement.[1] The *Labour Relations Act, 1995* requires that the employer meet with the union and try, in good faith, to reach an agreement. Failure to proceed in good faith is an unfair labour practice, as is any attempt to deal directly with the employees, which could result in sanctions by the Board against the employer.

The grant of certification continues the "freeze period" under the *Labour Relations Act, 1995*. During the freeze period all conditions of employment, including wages, hours and benefits are frozen, requiring the employer to conduct these matters in a "business as usual" manner.

The employer cannot unilaterally change an employment condition without the approval of the union. The freeze starts when the employer receives notice of the union's application for certification and, if the union is certified, lasts either until a collective agreement is signed or until the right to strike and lockout arises.

NEGOTIATIONS

Following receipt of notice to bargain from the union, arrangements are made to meet and commence bargaining.

The union bargaining team will usually consist of a professional from the union's full-time staff and a bargaining committee from the employees. These

---

[1]   In certain portions of the construction industry the employer will automatically become part of an employer's association and the association's collective agreement will apply.

committees are usually made up of from three to five persons representing the various different work groups contained within the bargaining unit.

Employers frequently give the bargaining committee time off work, sometimes paid and sometimes unpaid, to participate in the bargaining sessions. If the time is unpaid, many unions make up the employee's lost time.

The employer's bargaining team should consist of the most senior manager with immediate knowledge of the work involved. If the bargaining unit is a factory group, then this position is usually filled by the plant manager. The person with the responsibility for personnel matters should also be on the team. The most senior executive, in most cases, the company president, should not be at the bargaining table. It is better that this person be kept away from the battle at the table and available as someone the employer's team must leave to consult.

Most employers new to collective bargaining, and even many experienced employers, employ a professional to be their spokesperson at the table. Such professionals have the experience necessary to balance the union's full-time representative, a knowledge of the actual effect of the proposed clauses, and a knowledge of the union involved and how it works. Even large companies with full-time labour relations managers regularly employ outsiders to be their spokesperson as these outsiders have the advantage of diverse experience unobtainable by people working with one company. The use of such a professional is especially important when a first collective agreement is being negotiated. The language agreed to at this time may last decades. Realistically, employers can rarely retrieve something once it is agreed to.

Typically, at the first negotiating session, the union will present its demands, often in the form of a complete proposed agreement. If the negotiations are for a renewal of the collective agreement then the union will lead off with its list of proposed changes. At this session, company representatives should ask questions to clarify the union's demands but should not as yet respond to them.

After this first meeting the company's committee will consult with other people in management, including the senior executive, to develop its response. At the second meeting a complete proposed agreement should usually be tabled by the company. This proposal will adopt many of the provisions suggested by the union which are not in dispute though possibly with some changes in wording to ensure that the effect of these clauses are limited to their purposes. Where management proposed different or alternative clauses, the union will ask clarifying questions and then adjourn to consider these proposals.

At subsequent meetings, first the non-monetary issues affecting the rights of each party will be resolved to the extent possible, and then the monetary matters will be dealt with. Often, by the time the parties reach the monetary matters, as few as three or four non-monetary items remain in dispute. This process, including the first two meetings, typically takes five to seven meetings for the average-size factory unit if all is going well. However, for white-collar employees, especially professional groups such as teachers and nurses, and for large units (over 300), 10 and even 20 sessions are not unusual.

Every negotiated collective agreement must be ratified by the membership before it comes into effect. Ratification occurs when more than 50 per cent of those voting in a secret ballot vote cast their ballots in favour of the new collective agreement.

CONCILIATION

If the parties are unable to reach a collective agreement on their own, either party may apply for the assistance of an official from the Ministry of Labour to help them reach an agreement. This conciliation process is required by law before the union can strike or the employer can lock out its employees.

Conciliation officers are full-time government employees employed to assist parties in this situation. Since the union cannot strike until conciliation has failed, unions regularly invoke the process if they believe that one-to-one bargaining is not proving successful.

Once appointed the conciliation officer will meet with each of the parties to see if he or she can help. Usually, these meetings will be held at the same time but they will often start with each of the parties in a separate room. The conciliator will start by meeting separately with each party to determine its position. Once familiar with the situation, the conciliator may then bring the parties together to clarify any matters or to discuss outstanding issues. The conciliator may also keep the parties separate and go from one to the other trying to produce agreement.

In some cases, the conciliator promotes agreement by suggesting compromises that both sides agree to, or possibly, language that satisfies the concerns of both sides. In other cases, the conciliator may find that confidential positions disclosed to him or her indicate an overlap where agreement can be reached. For example, the union may be asking for a 1.5 per cent raise but is prepared to settle finally at 1.3 per cent; the company is offering 1.1 per cent but is also prepared to go to 1.3 per cent. Neither side, however, has told the other of its willingness to move for fear it will not produce a settlement and only weaken its position. The conciliator learns of their positions and then gets each, first separately then finally together, to agree on 1.3 per cent.

If all outstanding matters cannot be settled during conciliation, the conciliator reports the failure to settle to the Minister of Labour.

In the 1950s, at this point in the process if the dispute remained unsettled the Minister would often appoint a Conciliation Board. This Board would formally hear the positions of both parties and then issue a written decision outlining a possible settlement. The Board's decision was not binding and the process often included informal conciliation attempts by the Board members.

Today, the Conciliation Board is entirely unused. When the conciliation officer reports to the minister that an agreement has not been reached, the minister invariably issues a letter saying that no Conciliation Board will be appointed. The "no-board" letter triggers the countdown to the date the union can legally strike and the employer can legally lock out.

STRIKES AND LOCKOUTS

Seventeen days after the date of the no-board letter from the minister, the parties are permitted to engage in a strike or lockout.

In the days between the no-board and the legal strike date, bargaining will often continue. Usually, a mediator from the Ministry of Labour contacts the parties to offer assistance. This mediator may be the same person as the conciliator, now without a formal legal role in the process. The mediator's techniques are essentially the same as those used by the conciliator — only the existence of a rapidly approaching deadline is new.

The union, of course, has the option of not going on strike or of postponing the strike past the first legal day. Its decision in this regard will depend on many tactical considerations including, among other things, the state of bargaining and strike support among the employees.

Except in the construction industry, before a union can strike it must hold a strike vote and 50 per cent of those employees voting, must vote in favour of the strike. If a collective agreement is, or has been, in place, the strike vote must be taken not earlier than 30 days before the agreement expires or any time thereafter. If there has not yet been a collective agreement in place, the vote must be held on or after the day on which a conciliation officer is appointed. When possible, unions usually hold the vote early in the bargaining process in order to get it out of the way. At such an early stage, the employees, who are not facing any immediate negative consequences from voting for a strike, will almost invariably support the union with a strike mandate.

The employer may request that Ministry of Labour officials conduct a vote on its last offer. In order to take this step, a clearly set out final offer must be prepared. If the employees vote in favour of the offer, the Board has held that the union must conclude a collective agreement on the terms of the voted upon package. If, however, the offer is rejected, the employer must be prepared for the reality that under these circumstances concluding a collective agreement without a long strike will be almost impossible unless it increases its offer. The final offer vote can therefore be a double-edged sword. There can be only one such vote in any round of negotiations.

Strikes do not always involve the employees leaving work and picketing outside the employer's premises. Slowdowns, work to rule campaigns and other activities carried on jointly by employees that reduce the company's output, impair its efficiency or represent collective action, are strikes within the meaning of the *Labour Relations Act, 1995.*

Few employers ever lock out their employees. The few lockouts that do occur are usually a response to partial strikes, such as work to rule campaigns, or the result of a multi-employer agreement that if one is struck the others will lock out. In both cases, the purpose of the lockout is to maximize the effect on the employees and the union thus, hopefully, bringing them to terms.

Coincident with the right to lock out, the employer does get other rights as well. At this point, the freeze on working conditions that started with the application for certification, or, in renewal situations, with the expiry of the last agreement, finally comes to an end. The employer may now unilaterally change working conditions so long as it does not violate any other legal provisions. It may not, therefore, increase the pay of non-union supporters but not of union supporters, because that would be discriminatory and hence an unfair labour practice. Similarly, it may not fire the in-house union leadership without just cause.

The employer may, however, generally increase wages and other benefits. The increase cannot be tied to employees abandoning the union as that too would be an unfair labour practice. Nor can the new terms be discussed with the employees as the union remains their bargaining agent and any discussions must take place with the union. When taking any such action the employer should keep in mind that a collective agreement may eventually be backdated to cover this period of time.

The existence of a strike does not change the duty of both sides to continue to bargain in good faith. The Board has recognized, however, that fruitless discussions serve no purpose, so it has held it to be legal for one side to refuse to meet and bargain so long as the other side shows no willingness to change its position. Once an employer receives word from the union that it is willing to discuss a change in its position then the employer must return to the bargaining table until positions harden again or an agreement is reached. The employer too can bring about a return to the table by giving such notice to the union.

While on strike, employees retain their employment status and their right to a job for a six-month period.

While on strike employees may picket their employer for the purpose of informing other employees, customers and suppliers about the strike. A court decision early in 2002 also gave persons the right to engage in informational picketing about the strike almost anywhere they wished so long as in doing so they did not engage in unlawful behaviour. Unions are expected to use this to picket other locations operated by the same company, their employer's customers and even other companies that somehow assist the employer during the strike.

An application can be made to the courts to limit picketing action if it is out of control or includes illegal activities. The courts are, however, often reluctant to intervene.

FIRST CONTRACT ARBITRATION

If the parties are unable to settle the first collective agreement between them then either party may apply to the Board for an order that the contract be settled by binding arbitration. The *Labour Relations Act, 1995* instructs the Board to order arbitration if it finds that:

(a)　the employer has not really recognized the union;

(b)　the other side has taken an uncompromising position without reasonable justification;

(c)　the other side is not prepared to move the process along; or

(d)　any other reason the Board considers relevant.

An order to proceed to arbitration ends any strike that may be in progress and prevents strike action.

The possibility of an arbitrated agreement puts increased emphasis on the need to conduct bargaining professionally. For a number of reasons, unions are tempted to use the arbitration process when it is available rather than make unpopular compromises to reach a deal directly. By conducting bargaining properly the employer ensures that arbitration is not made available.

TERMINATION OF BARGAINING RIGHTS

Each year, approximately 100 applications are made to the Board to decertify or terminate bargaining rights. Of those that are made, many are a prelude to an application for certification by another union. Certification applications directly by other unions are possible whenever a termination application can be made but for various internal union reasons the two-step procedure is sometimes used.

An application to the Board to terminate a trade union's right to represent employees may be made by an employer only where the trade union fails to give notice to bargain within 60 days of certification or of the expiry of a previous agreement, or, having given notice, fails to commence bargaining within 60 days, or having commenced bargaining, allows 60 days to lapse without attempting to continue bargaining.

When such an application is made, the Board will usually turn it down if there is any apparent continuing union interest in the bargaining unit. If there is any doubt, the Board will order a vote. As a result, successful applications by employers are very rare.

Employees may also bring a termination application under such circumstances. Additionally, employees may bring a termination application under the following conditions:[2]

(1) If no collective agreement is signed within one year of certification so long as:
(a) 30 days have passed since the no-board letter, if there was one, or,
(b) if there has been a strike,
(i) six months have passed since it started, or
(ii) seven months have passed since the no-board letter.
(2) Where the parties are or have been party to a collective agreement, termination applications can be made during a period that starts with the beginning of the last three months of the agreement and ends either with the expiry of the agreement or with the appointment of a conciliation officer, whichever occurs later.
(3) Where a conciliation officer has been appointed in a situation where the parties are bargaining for a second or subsequent collective agreement, any time after 12 months from the appointment of the officer.

Employees must make an application for termination on specific Board Forms. Forms and Information Bulletins describing the process and required documentation are available on the Board's website, online: <http://www.olrb.gov.on.ca>. The application must be accompanied by proof, usually a signed statement, that at least 40 per cent of the employees in the bargaining unit support the application. If the application meets these conditions and over 50 per cent of those voting support termination, then the Board will terminate the union's bargaining rights. The Board will reject the employees' application if it believes it was generated or influenced by the employer.

Employers are required to post certain documentation from the Board, including a copy of the application for termination and a form explaining employee rights to bring an application to terminate bargaining rights. Employers are also required to complete and return certain forms to the Board, whether or not they decide to formally intervene in the application.

SALE OF A BUSINESS

The *Labour Relations Act, 1995* requires that when an employer sells, leases or otherwise disposes of a business (including via a bankruptcy) the union's rights follow the business. If the company and the union have a collective agreement,

---

[2] Certain very technical and rarely used timing rules have been left out to keep this description simple.

then the new owner picks up the agreement as it is. If the parties are bargaining, or are at the point in time where the union could give notice to bargain, then the union can give notice to bargain to the new employer.

Whether or not a particular transaction represents a "sale of a business" occasionally causes some trouble. It does not matter whether the sale is structured as a share or asset purchase if the business is changing hands, but it is not always clear what constitutes "the business". The Board has held, for example, that where a lease is the key item to carrying on a particular kind of business then the sale of the lease is a sale of the business.

If the new owner substantially changes the character of the business the Board may, on an application made within 60 days of the sale, terminate the union's bargaining rights. Changing a gravel dump into a recreational swimming area is just such a substantial change.

Occasionally, problems result because the new owner mixes the new business into an existing business that may have no union, or a different union. For example, such a mixing of the two enterprises will usually be considered to have occurred when employees are intermingled. In these circumstances an application can be made to the Board for a decision, possibly preceded by a vote of the employees, as to what union, if any, should represent the employees.

Chapter 8

The Collective Agreement

THE BASIC PROVISIONS OF AN AGREEMENT*

The provisions of each collective agreement vary with the nature, size and complexity of the industry and the concerns that the parties bring to the negotiations. For example, the agreement between Hydro One and its union is the size of a small city telephone directory because it deals with many working conditions for numerous occupations. However, most white-collar and industrial agreements have a common base, to which is added the special clauses that are required. The following sections deal with the typical provisions of such collective agreements.

Recognition

The recognition clause sets out a description of the bargaining unit, which is the group of employees that the trade union represents and for whom it bargains. The union is entitled to represent the unit specified by the Ontario Labour Relations Board (the "Board") in its certificate, and neither side can insist upon changing it. Either party can, however, propose changes in the bargaining unit description so long as a dispute over these changes is not allowed to reach the point of a strike or lockout.

Union Security and Checkoff

Ontario law now provides that, if the union so requests, an employer must agree to a provision in a collective agreement that calls for a mandatory union dues deduction from all employees. There remains only the issue as to whether all employees will be formally required to become members of the trade union. While many trade unions insist on compulsory membership, non-negotiable,

---

* For a more complete description of Collective Agreement provisions, see S. Saxe and B. McLean, *Collective Agreement Handbook: A Guide for Employers and Employees, Third Edition* (Toronto: Canada Law Book, 2010).

compulsory dues deduction has made major disputes over "union security clauses" a thing of the past.

Union Rights

This clause is often titled the "relationship" or the "plant committee" clause. The major provision usually found under one of these headings requires that the employer recognize certain union executives as having day to day authority to speak for the union. The clause regularly goes on to provide that the employer will give these executives time during working hours to pursue the settlement of employee grievances. The clause will also usually require that the employer allow a full-time union representative to come onto its premises for the purpose of meeting with local union officers and participating in the resolution of grievances.

Another common provision requires that bulletin boards on the employer's premises be designated for union use. The right to post materials on the bulletin boards will sometimes be subject to prior approval by the company.

Management Rights

It is generally accepted that management retains those rights that predate the arrival of a trade union except to the extent the collective agreement specifically limits the company's authority. Nonetheless, a management rights clause clarifies and lends support to management's ongoing role after the arrival of a union.

The management rights clause provides an opportunity to ensure that the company has certain rights which it would not otherwise have or that might otherwise be in doubt. As an example, employers generally want to include the right to require that employees get a medical examination from a doctor of the company's choosing where a claim on medical grounds is being made.

Every year, more and more areas once considered to have been within management's prerogative are being raised by unions as topics for negotiation. The most common of these include:

(a) **Closedowns.** Unions are seeking limits on the right of a company to transfer its operations and even on the right to go out of business. In the case of transfers, the union's major concern is that the company not move to any place where the union's bargaining rights would not follow. In the case of discontinuance, the unions are seeking substantial severance benefits as well as requirements that companies planning to discontinue an operation fully disclose their reasons.

(b) **Excluded Persons and Unit Work.** The union will wish to guarantee that only employees who are within the bargaining unit will be allowed to do work regularly assigned to the unit. Such a provision ensures that, so long as the employer has work of that nature, bargaining unit members will do it and, thus, guarantees that the unit will be as large as possible. A common compromise restricts only supervisors and more senior people from doing bargaining unit work and even then allows them to do so only in emergencies or for instruction purposes.

(c) **Contracting Out.** The union will also want to limit the employer's right to send the work out to be done by other enterprises. Again, the union's goal is to ensure work for its members. Employers usually try vigorously to preserve this right. A common compromise prohibits contracting out if it will result in any employee being laid off.

(d) **Technological Change.** As a further protection for the bargaining unit, unions seek an involvement in the introduction of any new technologies within the company. Commonly, unions will require that they be notified in advance of the introduction of any major new equipment so that they can bargain with the company about any results that flow from the planned changes. Unions also regularly seek an assurance that when such changes are made, existing employees will be guaranteed their jobs.

Grievance and Arbitration Procedure

The *Labour Relations Act, 1995* requires that disputes (*i.e.*, grievances) about the interpretation, administration or application of the collective agreement be submitted to binding third party arbitration.

Collective agreements inevitably provide for pre-arbitration discussion of such grievances at various levels of the union and the company. Typically, such discussions are required first between the individual and the foreperson; then between the individual, the local union official and the plant manager; and finally between the individual, the local union official, a full-time union representative and the most senior level of management. Large employers often establish committees for the last stage of the discussions. If this procedure for discussing the grievance does not resolve the problem, then the matter proceeds to arbitration by an outside arbitrator or board of arbitration.

Each step in this pre-arbitration grievance procedure may have a time limit attached to it. Such provisions will limit the number of days the employee or union has to complain in the first place and then to proceed from one step to the next. Limits may also be set out governing the length of time management is allowed for a reply. The *Labour Relations Act, 1995* provides that these time limits are guidelines only and not absolute rules unless this provision of the Act is specifically excluded. If such a limit is passed, an arbitrator hearing the matter is given authority to decide what result, if any, should flow from missing the limit.

At one time, almost all collective agreements called for arbitration by three-person boards appointed by the parties when they required them. The boards would consist of a company representative, a union representative and an agreed upon neutral chairperson chosen by the two representatives. Recently single arbitrators chosen directly by the parties have become the norm.

Provisions under the *Labour Relations Act, 1995* also allow either party to refer a grievance for arbitration by an arbitrator appointed by the Minister of Labour.

The decision of an arbitrator or a board of arbitration is binding upon the parties and cannot be appealed. If, however, the arbitrator makes an unreasonable error in applying the law to the facts at hand, an application can be made to the courts to review the arbitrator's determination of law. The court will generally defer to the arbitrator's expertise in labour law and his or her interpretation of the facts.

It is established law that all labour disputes that arise out of the collective agreement are within the exclusive jurisdiction of an arbitrator. In other words, an individual employee or union cannot sue their employer in court over a matter arising out of the collective agreement (unlike the non-unionized employment environment which is primarily dealt with in the courts). In any attempt to do so, the court will refuse to hear the matter and require the parties to seek arbitration as per the dispute resolution provision in the collective agreement.

Just Cause, Discharge and Discipline

Every collective agreement is deemed to require that any discipline or discharge of an employee be for just cause. (This topic is discussed fully below at "Discharge and Discipline of Unionized Employees".) In discipline and discharge cases, arbitrators have the authority, pursuant to the *Labour Relations Act, 1995*, not only to uphold or repeal management's decision but also to substitute a different penalty, unless the collective agreement specifically sets out the penalty that is to follow an infraction.

Seniority

Even relatively simple collective agreements for small operations often contain extensive seniority provisions. "Seniority" means the length of time the employee has been with the company. Seniority clauses seek, at the very least, to ensure an employee security of future employment at the company. They do this primarily by requiring that the company grant the greatest degree of security of employment to the employees who have been with the company the longest.

The most common seniority provision requires that any lay-off be in reverse order of seniority. This requirement can be on a department-wide or a plant-wide basis, with unions usually seeking that it be a plant-wide determination. Such provisions will also require that a recall to work be made in the order of most senior first. In agreeing to such clauses, as with all seniority clauses, employers will wish to ensure that the clause allows them to consider not just seniority but also the skill and ability of the employees in question. For example, in some collective agreements the company retains the right in a lay-off situation to keep those employees who have certain specific skills that the company needs in order to keep the operation going.

Seniority may also be the trigger for the other rights found in the collective agreement. Provision is often made for a probationary period, typically 60 days, during which the employee does not acquire seniority rights. Probationary employees are usually excluded from certain benefit coverage, such as holiday pay and life insurance.

Unions also seek to apply seniority to promotion and transfer decisions within the bargaining unit. Provisions in the agreement may require that the employer post a notice of any vacancy within the unit and choose from the applicants on the basis of seniority. In this situation especially, employers will want to be sure that they have the right to consider not only the seniority but also the skill and the ability of the applicants. Various compromises can be arrived at. For example, the clause can require that seniority will be considered only where the employee's skills and abilities are relatively equal. A more pro-trade union compromise will require that seniority will govern so long as the employee has the minimum required skill and ability.

Other seniority clauses will usually set out the circumstances under which an employee loses seniority. This provision can be crucial as it may define the point at which the employer-employee relationship is finally at an end. In a lay-off situation, for example, the agreement may specify that the employee retains his or her seniority rights for 12 months. If that is the case, then the employer is required to recall that employee should work become available at any time during that 12-month period.

Strikes and Lockouts

In Ontario, strikes and lockouts during the term of a collective agreement are prohibited. It is common for a provision restating this requirement of the *Labour Relations Act, 1995* to be found in the agreement.

Hours of Work and Overtime

Most agreements contain a provision which sets out the standard number of hours of work in a day and in a week, and may specify, as well, the starting and stopping time of the regular work day. Outside of the regular work hours, the agreement will require that overtime, either at time and one-half or double time, be paid. Double time is usually reserved for work done on Sundays or on statutory public holidays.

The overtime provisions of a collective agreement may also limit management's right to require that employees work overtime. Other provisions in the hours of work clause may limit the employer's right to introduce new shifts or may call for premium rates of pay if such shifts are introduced.

Common too is a clause that requires that if employees are regularly scheduled for work and show up as required, or are called in to work by the company, they will be paid for a minimum of two to four hours, even if the company does not require them.

Rest periods, wash-up periods and lunch periods are usually specifically set out.

Paid Holidays and Vacation

The collective agreement will specify that employees be given a number of paid holidays each year. Currently, provisions requiring 11 to 13 such holidays are common. These paid holidays generally include the nine public holidays provided for by the *Employment Standards Act*. The agreement may allow the employer the right to require that employees work on a paid holiday in which case the employer may be required to pay double time and give another day as a paid holiday in lieu of the holiday worked.

Employers should seek a clause which clarifies the circumstances under which they are required to pay holiday pay. This clause should, at the very least, specify that employees must have been at work on the working day preceding and the working day following the paid holiday in order to get holiday pay. Such a provision ensures that employees do not abuse the holiday pay requirement.

A vacation provision will also be found in most collective agreements. Commonly, the provision provides for an increasing scale of vacation entitlement. A two-week vacation with pay may be granted to employees with from one to five years of service, while employees with five to 10 years of service may get three weeks and employees with over 10 years, four weeks. While the *Employment Standards Act* requires that vacation pay be a percentage of earnings received during the previous year many collective agreements simply require that the employee be paid regular wages for the vacation period.

Unions may also seek a requirement that the employer post a vacation schedule or make vacation arrangements with employees by a fixed date, usually a day early in the spring.

Leaves of Absence

Collective agreements regularly provide for bereavement leave, jury leave and discretionary leave.

Bereavement leave provisions will typically allow the employee up to three days to attend the funeral of a close relative. The clause will usually define exactly who is a close relative. Where the employee cannot attend the funeral for reasons such as the distance from the employee's current residence, the clause will often allow a one-day paid leave for the purpose of mourning. Employers should ensure that the employee is entitled to a leave that covers only the day of and before and after the funeral so that when a funeral takes place on a non-working day that day becomes one of the three days of the leave. Wages, of course, should be payable only for working days missed.

Jury duty leave provisions usually ensure that the employee suffers no loss of wages by attending to jury duty. This is accomplished by paying the employee for the lost time and requiring that the employee turn over to the employer any jury duty pay received.

The discretionary leave of absence provisions allow employees to seek from the company a leave for any good reason. The company has a discretion to grant or refuse the leave but this discretion is often limited by a requirement that it be exercised on a reasonable and good-faith basis.

Some unions are also now seeking to include a paid education leave provision. Such a leave is usually of approximately one week's duration and is for the purpose of attending seminars on labour relations matters conducted by the union. As well as providing for employee leaves, this clause may require that the employer make an ongoing contribution of, for example, one cent per hour per employee to a fund designed to cover the cost of the company's employees attending such seminars.

Following introduction of an emergency leave provision in the *Employment Standards Act*, the parties to collective agreements are often seeking to integrate the Act's provisions into the collective agreement rights.

Regardless of what is included in the collective agreement, employees are entitled to the leaves of absences provided for in the *Employment Standards Act*, such as pregnancy leave, parental leave, reservist leave, organ donor leave, *etc.* (see the full discussion on statutory leaves of absences in Chapter 1).

Wages and Benefits

Of course, one of the union's primary goals in the collective agreement is to achieve a wage increase for its members. In the inflationary era of the past, one of the most contentious issues at the bargaining table is often the union's demand for regular wage increases tied to the increase in the cost of living. Since the turn of the century, very stable inflation rates have made such concerns much less common.

Called a "cost of living allowance", or "COLA" clause, such provisions typically require that the employer give a wage increase every quarter or every half year in an amount that is related to the increase in the Consumer Price Index for the period in question.[1] The amount of the wage increase can be directly proportional to the increase in the Consumer Price Index or can be related to the Consumer Price Index change in such a way so as to only partially cover the increase. Sometimes a COLA clause will be limited in its effect to increases above an established level or percentage. Conversely, the COLA clause may be limited to a specified maximum.

The inclusion of a COLA clause in a collective agreement can create serious problems for companies that must do long-range costs of labour forecasting. Where, for example, the company's product must be priced substantially in advance of the date of manufacture, the existence of a COLA clause places in some doubt the labour cost component of the product. In any event, the need to establish in advance what the likely cost of the clause will be for the purposes of determining its effect in a collective agreement can create a real disagreement between the parties not only as to its inclusion but as to how beneficial it is. For example, the company's costing of the clause must necessarily be based on pessimistic assumptions and so in a given case they may assume that the clause is going to cost them 13 per cent. The union on the other hand only wants to count what it is sure about getting, hence, in the same situation it may value the clause as being worth 7 per cent. In the result, the parties are a full 6 per cent apart in the evaluation of the benefit that such a clause is to the employees. Nonetheless, high rates of inflation in the early 1980s made COLA clauses much more common. By the mid 1990s, such clauses were often left inoperative or deleted.

Commonly found benefits include life insurance, death and dismemberment insurance, disability insurance and extended medical benefits such as dental or vision care. Pension plans are also regularly sought. In each of these cases the plan represents a cost to the employer which must be calculated in determining the cost of the collective agreement package. In making its calculation, the employer must keep in mind that, once granted, the benefits will be hard to withdraw and that their costs are usually tied to the wage level. In the result, future wage increases will produce an increased cost for the benefit package, which will be a real expense for the employer, but one that will be hard to get the union to recognize.

Duration

The *Labour Relations Act, 1995* requires that a collective agreement be for at least a duration of one year. Most collective agreements in Ontario today are for two or three years. It is rare for agreements to be for longer than three years'

---

[1] Statistics Canada is responsible for publishing monthly updates of the Consumer Price Index. Updates are available, online: <http://www40.statcan.gc.ca/z01/cs0001-eng.htm>.

duration, particularly as there are complex impacts on the union's right to represent employees if the agreement lasts longer than three years.

DISCHARGE AND DISCIPLINE OF UNIONIZED EMPLOYEES

As noted above, collective agreements require that the discharge and discipline of employees covered by the agreement be "for just cause". Agreements must also contain, by law, a provision that any unsettled dispute regarding their application, administration or interpretation be referred to independent arbitration. The result of these two provisions is that employer discipline and discharge of employees is subject to review by an outside party or parties in the form of an arbitration board to see if there was just cause.

It therefore becomes important to determine what arbitrators will do in discipline and discharge cases. Since these collective agreement provisions have been common for over 50 years, a large number of decided cases are available for review and guidance in making this determination.

Types of Discipline

Unless the collective agreement specifically provides that unusual types of discipline are permissible, either generally or in specific areas, arbitrators will usually limit employer discipline to warnings, suspensions and discharge.

Monetary penalties (in other words, fines) will usually be allowed only in situations where they, in fact, compensate the employer for a loss that it has directly incurred. As an example, fines will sometimes be allowed as a disciplinary response for defective workmanship. They are usually not allowed, however, as a response for being late.

Reductions in an employee's seniority have rarely been allowed unless specifically provided for. Demotions, however, have been allowed for quality of work-related disciplinary problems. Arbitrators have upheld demotions for repeated work negligence, poor work attitudes, lack of effort and for falsification of product records.

Where collective agreements provide a specific penalty for a specific infraction, arbitrators will probably uphold the penalty so long as they find the infraction has been proven. In such cases the arbitrator's normal authority under the *Labour Relations Act, 1995* to substitute a different penalty than that imposed by the employer is set aside because of the agreement's specific language. The employer, however, must have consistently applied the penalties set out in the agreement. If an arbitrator finds that in other cases the employer has varied the penalty, the arbitrator is likely to hold that his or her discretion is no less than that of the employer.

Selecting Appropriate Discipline

The first rule of discipline imposed by arbitrators is that it should be progressive. Arbitrators want to see a history of discipline progressing from warnings to suspensions and only finally to discharge. The number of times that discipline must issue at each step of this ladder, and, indeed the number of steps on the ladder that must be taken, depend on the nature of the infraction and a number of other factors arbitrators consider when reviewing the employer's selection of a disciplinary response.

The following is a standard list of factors widely considered by arbitrators in reviewing the level of discipline imposed. Since a case that goes before an arbitrator or arbitration board will have these considerations applied to it, employers should consider them in advance to increase the chance that they will not be overruled by the arbitration.

PROVOCATION

If the employee was provoked into the action for which discipline was imposed, arbitrators may completely exonerate the behaviour. At the very least, arbitrators will consider that the provocation greatly reduces the level of penalty that can be imposed. The nature and source of the provocation is important. If, for example, a supervisor addresses an employee using a racial slur, the employee's subsequent refusal to obey the supervisor's instructions will probably be completely excused. On the other hand, if an employee assaults a fellow employee for calling him or her a name, some disciplinary result is likely to be upheld.

PREMEDITATION

If the disciplinary offence was spur of the moment behaviour and not premeditated, arbitrators may reduce the discipline to a level they consider appropriate.

SPECIAL ECONOMIC HARDSHIP

Arbitrators have held that the severity of discipline must be considered in terms of the actual individual being penalized. This rule is especially applied in discharge cases. Such special economic hardship may result for older, unskilled employees who will find it difficult to locate any other employment, for example, a 63-year-old janitor.

UNIFORM ENFORCEMENT

Arbitrators require that similar cases be treated in a similar fashion. Where, for example, two employees both take an unauthorized three-day leave of absence and one receives a two-day suspension while the other receives a four-day suspension, the arbitrator will likely reduce the second penalty to a two-day suspension. Where the employees are treated differently for legitimate reasons, for example, a very different past record, the employer should document this fact. It should be prepared to show the arbitrator that these differences were considered at the time discipline was handed out and were the reason for the variance in the discipline. The rule is applied to similar situations even if they happen at different times. Employers must, therefore, develop a consistent disciplinary approach and be prepared to justify any instance of different treatment. The argument that the employer has imposed a lesser penalty in the past for the same cause is becoming one of the most common reasons given by arbitrators for reducing the level of discipline selected by the employer.

CIRCUMSTANCES NEGATING INTENT

Anything that shows that the employee may not have understood what he or she was doing will be considered by the arbitrator. Common considerations include the possibility that the employee misunderstood the situation, especially where insubordination is involved, or that the employee was under extreme personal stress at the time and hence "not thinking right". Even drunkenness has been considered as a factor under this heading. Because of this consideration, arbitrators require that companies give an employee a chance to explain his or her actions before discipline is imposed.

SERIOUSNESS OF THE OFFENCE

Arbitrators consider the seriousness of the offence in terms of the company's policies and obligations. Where, for example, an employee breaks a dress or appearance code, arbitrators will consider whether the employee was in public view and whether the regulation was safety related. If neither is the case, arbitrators are reluctant to uphold anything beyond the least severe forms of discipline.

EMPLOYEE APOLOGIES

Where arbitrators have found that the employee's wrongdoing has been proven, they generally hold it against the employee who has failed to apologize. If the employee has apologized and has admitted the wrongdoing that is often one of the reasons given for lessening the penalty.

EMPLOYEE'S PREVIOUS RECORD

As the existence of the disciplinary ladder of warnings, suspension and discharge indicates, arbitrators consider the employee's previous disciplinary record to be very important in determining the appropriate discipline for a current misdeed. The underlying arbitral theory of discipline is that its primary purpose is to correct the employee's performance with the final result of discharging the employee only when all else has failed or where the infraction is so bad as to not reasonably allow continued employment.

In order to consider an employee's record there must be a current incident for which discipline is being considered. The weight given to previous incidents will depend on their number, how closely spaced they are, their severity and their relevance to the issue in question. For previous matters to be considered they must have been brought to the employee's attention at the time they happened.

CONDONATION

If the employer has in the past condoned the kind of behaviour in question, by either this or other employees, it cannot suddenly change its approach and discipline a particular employee. Where a change of approach is contemplated, the employer should make this known in advance. If, for example, a company has tolerated a practice of lateness on the part of its employees and wishes to bring this to a stop, it should first notify the employees of the change in policy before disciplining any employee for being late.

REHABILITATIVE POTENTIAL

If an arbitrator feels that an employee is likely to correct a bad behaviour pattern then severe discipline, particularly discharge, is not likely to be upheld. This rule is applied most commonly in lateness and absenteeism situations. The arbitrator may create a probationary period during which, if there is no improvement, the employer can terminate the employee.

COMPASSION

If all else fails to save the employee, a number of arbitrators have held that if there is compassion available it should be exercised in the employee's favour.

Specific Offences

As can be seen from the previous section there are many factors which must be weighed and considered in choosing a level of discipline for a particular employee and a particular situation. As well as those previously discussed factors, general arbitral attitudes toward specific kinds of offences are important in determining what level of discipline arbitrators will uphold. For the purposes of this chapter, these attitudes will be classified into three groups.

For minor offences, arbitrators require repeated warnings before they will uphold a suspension, and a number of suspensions before they will uphold a discharge. For middle-level offences, arbitrators may require a warning before a suspension and possibly a number of suspensions before a discharge. Finally, for the most serious offences, arbitrators will allow suspension and possibly even discharge as an immediate response.

ABSENTEEISM

To be the subject of discipline at all, absenteeism must be without permission and without justifiable excuse. Where there is an excuse but the employee has failed to notify the employer, if required to do so, discipline may be allowed for that cause. Employer responses to justifiable absenteeism are discussed under the heading "Non-Disciplinary Discharge and Demotion" below.

LEAVING WORK WITHOUT PERMISSION

This offence is treated much like absenteeism.

LATENESS

Lateness is possibly the most minor of offences. A substantial history of warnings will usually be required before more serious discipline will be upheld.

THEFT

Theft is considered a serious offence and usually supports immediate discharge as a penalty. Arbitrators will usually reduce a discharge only if the article removed is of nominal value and if the employee has a long, clean record. Arbitrators have tended to distinguish borrowing an item without permission from theft. Where the employee intends to return the item, the action falls within the "borrowing" category and arbitrators will usually reduce a discharge to a substantial suspension.

FALSIFICATION OF PRODUCTION RECORDS

Falsification of production records is usually considered a middle-level offence, unless it results in a gain to the employee, as where there is an incentive plan, in which case it is treated as theft. The consequences for the employer are an important consideration when arbitrators are deciding on the appropriate level of discipline.

FALSIFICATION OF EMPLOYMENT APPLICATION FORMS

Such conduct is considered a middle-level offence and again arbitrators will look to the effect of the falsification on the employer. Some cases have held that a warning on the application form that discharge will result from a falsification strengthens the employer's ability to so respond.

FIGHTING

Assaulting a supervisor or other member of management is considered a serious offence. Fighting with a fellow employee is usually considered less serious.

POOR WORK PERFORMANCE

If an employee's poor work performance is through lack of ability, it will generally not be considered a disciplinary matter. When it can be shown that the poor performance is the result of a lack of effort, it is considered to be a minor level of offence. In such cases, arbitrators require not only a series of warnings before more serious discipline will be upheld, they also require that it be clear that the standard required was made known to the employee and can be shown to be reasonable.

CARELESSNESS

Arbitrators recognize that accidents do happen and cannot be considered anybody's fault. Where an employee's work habits have become so careless or negligent that they must be rectified, arbitrators require of the employer the same progressive discipline as in poor work performance cases.

PERSONAL APPEARANCE

Arbitrators are reluctant to uphold any discipline for failure to meet rules regarding personal appearance until it is shown that the rule is based upon a health and safety requirement, the need for sanitation in the workplace or legitimate concern regarding business image. Violations of such rules are considered minor offences unless, as is frequently the case, there are special considerations.

INSUBORDINATION

Depending on the circumstances, insubordination may be a middle-level or occasionally a serious-level offence. The reasonableness of the action being required by the employer is considered. Where an employee believes that he or she has some right, possibly under the collective agreement, to refuse to do the task in question, arbitrators have held that in most circumstances the employee must obey the instruction and pursue any dispute through the grievance procedure in the collective agreement. This is called the "work now, grieve later" rule.

DRUGS AND ALCOHOL

While using drugs or alcohol at work may be a cause for discipline in certain circumstances, employers will want to proceed with caution in this area. If the employee can establish that he or she is suffering from an addiction to drugs or alcohol, he or she is now suffering from a disability and pursuant to the *Human Rights Code*, the employer will be under a duty to accommodate the employee up to undue hardship. Unless the employee is in a safety sensitive position, random drug and alcohol testing will rarely be supported by an arbitrator in Ontario. Employers must therefore deal with any employees found to consume drugs or alcohol at work on a case-by-case basis. If the consumption is a one-time incident and the employee has an otherwise clean record, the offence will be considered a minor offence. For an employee who routinely abuses or deals drugs or alcohol in the workplace and either denies an addiction or refuses to attend rehabilitation treatment, the series of offences will be considered a serious offence, and after appropriate progressive discipline, may be subject to discharge. In either case, this area of employee behaviour requires a carefully documented progressive discipline approach.

Probationary Employees

Most collective agreements establish a period of time at the commencement of employment during which an employee is considered probationary. Depending on the specific wording of the collective agreement, discipline and discharge during this period may not be reviewable by arbitration at all or, may be reviewed under arbitral approaches which allow management a much wider discretion than is otherwise the case.

Non-Disciplinary Discharge and Demotion

Since the primary purpose of discipline is to correct the employee's improper behaviour, it follows that where the underlying causes are such that correction is not possible, discipline is not appropriate. This does not mean, however, that employers are stuck with poor employees when the cause for their unacceptable level of performance is not their fault. Arbitrators will allow discharge or demotion where absolutely required. In such cases it must usually be shown that the problem is not about to disappear. Some of the common reasons and arbitral approaches to non-disciplinary discharge and demotion are set out below:

INCOMPETENCE

Employers who have probationary periods in their collective agreements should try to ensure that incompetent employees do not complete the probationary period. Once an employee has passed the probationary period, the employer must be able to prove the incompetence clearly and to prove that the standard being required is a reasonable one in order to fire him or her for incompetence. If this can be done, arbitrators prefer transferring the employee to a job the employee is capable of, if such a job exists, and if the transfer is not prohibited by other provisions of the collective agreement, such as the seniority provisions.

DISABILITY

Again, arbitrators prefer transferring employees who have suffered a disability that interferes with their job performance. Arbitrators will uphold a termination only where no job the employee is capable of doing is available and the employer shows that it cannot accommodate the workplace to assist the employee in performing a job. The provisions of the *Human Rights Code* to accommodate the disabled must be considered and will be applied by the arbitrator.

INNOCENT ABSENTEEISM OR LATENESS

At some point, arbitrators acknowledge that repeated lateness or absenteeism, even where it is through no fault of the employee, becomes cause for discharge. Non-disciplinary warnings must precede a discharge and arbitrators will usually reinstate the employee if the employee can show that the underlying cause has been remedied. The most common example is that of an employee whose repeated illnesses have led to a bad record of absenteeism. Where such an employee is able to produce medical evidence at the arbitration that he or she will now be able to attend work regularly, arbitrators will usually reinstate and impose a probationary period. During the probationary period the employer can terminate the employee if the employee's absenteeism rate climbs above that of the company's average rate.

Chapter 9

Privacy Law[*]

INTRODUCTION

With the federal government's enactment in 2001 of the *Personal Information Protection and Electronic Documents Act* ("PIPEDA"), there was considerable momentum towards implementing personal information protection laws across Canada ("Privacy Law").

At that time, there was a discernible awakening of public concern over the facility with which organizations, including employers, could use high technology to obtain information about individuals and the resulting uses that could be made of that information.

Modelled loosely on the data privacy directives passed by the European Union in the 1990s, PIPEDA was to be the watershed event in Privacy Law in Canada, where the provinces would follow suit in enacting similar legislation or adopting PIPEDA itself for provincial application.

The problem that has plagued PIPEDA in its first decade as law is not in its design or administration, though neither has been perfect. Rather, PIPEDA suffers from a constitutionally-limited scope which it inherits from its creator — the Government of Canada.

PIPEDA APPLICATION TO EMPLOYEES LIMITED

While PIPEDA applies to all "commercial activities" of organizations in Canada, it only applies to employee personal information of federally-regulated employers, such as inter-provincial transportation companies, national banks and telecommunications companies.[1]

To encourage the creation and harmonization of provincial privacy protection laws, PIPEDA exempts organizations in any province in which the legislature has passed legislation "substantially similar" to PIPEDA. This exemption,

---

*   This chapter was prepared by Jonathan Cocker of Baker & McKenzie, Toronto.

[1]   Under the Canadian Constitution, the provincial governments, and not the federal government, have the jurisdiction to regulate most private sector companies located in that province.

however, applies only to personal information which has been collected, used or disclosed solely within a province which has enacted qualifying Privacy Law.

Further, this available exemption has fostered few Privacy Law initiatives from provincial governments, who understand that PIPEDA cannot be lawfully extended to areas of provincial legislative control, such as employee Privacy Law.

LIMITED PROVINCIAL RESPONSE TO PIPEDA

To date, only three provinces have passed Privacy Laws. Quebec was first to implement Privacy Law, which it did in 1994, prior to the passage of PIPEDA. The Quebec legislation has since been deemed to be "substantially similar" to PIPEDA by the federal government.

In 2004, the provinces of British Columbia and Alberta passed similar Privacy Laws: the British Columbia *Personal Information Protection Act* ("B.C. PIPA") and the Alberta *Personal Information Protection Act* ("Alberta PIPA"). These Acts have deviated from some of the more onerous requirements under PIPEDA, introducing greater flexibility in the application of Privacy Law. The B.C. PIPA and the Alberta PIPA have also been deemed "substantially similar" by the federal government.

Curiously, the Ontario government introduced its own draft Privacy Law in 2002, the *Privacy of Personal Information Act*, only to then allow Privacy Law to fall off the legislative agenda, where it has remained ever since.

PERSONAL INFORMATION PROTECTED

Privacy Law is directed towards the protection of "personal information", including the personal information of employees. All information which identifies, or can be used to identify, a specific individual is covered, save for a limited set of exemptions. Most notably, an employee's name, business address and position within an organization are not considered personal information under Privacy Law.

The Privacy Commissioner of Canada, however, has indicated that, under PIPEDA, an employee's email address is not exempt from personal information and, therefore, falls under the protections under PIPEDA. The provincial privacy commissions have not accepted this position.

Any collection, use or disclosure of personal information on an anonymous, collective or generic basis, so as to not reveal an individual's identity, does not fall within the definition of personal information and does not attract the application of Privacy Law.

COLLECTION, USE AND DISCLOSURE

Collection of Personal Information

Privacy Law places limits on the methods of collection of personal information. Organizations are not permitted to collect personal information indiscriminately, but must only collect information, with the individual's consent, that is required for legitimate purposes.

There are some specific exclusions to the consent requirement for personal information collection. The emergency collection of information that is clearly in the interests of the individual, for instance, does not require consent. Similarly, information used in an investigation of a possible breach of an agreement or contravention of law may also be collected without consent.[2]

Use and Disclosure

Personal information under Privacy Law must not be used or disclosed for legitimate purposes other than those for which it was collected, except with the consent of the individual or as required by law. Furthermore, personal information may only be retained as long as necessary for the fulfilment of these purposes.

Information used to make a decision about an individual must be retained long enough to allow the individual access to the information after the decision is made. Once the personal information is no longer required for business or legal purposes, that information must be destroyed.

Where personal information that has been collected is to be used for a purpose not previously identified, the new purpose shall be identified and consented to by the individual prior to use.

Similar to collection, personal information may be used or disclosed by an organization without an individual's consent in a few specific instances, such as in the event of an emergency, where health or security is threatened or where it is used in a legal investigation.

PRIVACY PRINCIPLES

Privacy Law incorporates, either directly or indirectly, the Canadian Standards Association's *Model Code for the Protection of Personal Information*. The Model Code contains a number of principles regarding the obligations of organizations with respect to personal information. Some of the more relevant principles include:

---

[2] The nature of the exemptions to the consent requirement for collection, use and disclosure does somewhat vary under the different federal and provincial Privacy Laws.

The "Accuracy Principle"

An organization is accountable for personal information under its control. A person must be designated by each organization as responsible for ensuring that the information in its possession is accurate.

The "Consent Principle"

The requirement to obtain the consent of the individual for the purposes of collection, use and disclosure of personal information is described as the "Consent Principle".

Under the Consent Principle, individuals must generally be advised of the purposes for which their personal information is to be used so that they may provide informed consent to the processing of their personal information. At a minimum, a request for consent should refer to: (i) the nature of the information to be collected, used or disclosed; (ii) the specific uses to which the information will be put by the parties receiving it; and (iii) the identity of the parties to whom information is to be disclosed, as applicable.

Further, an organization must not require an individual to consent to the use of personal information beyond the legitimate purposes communicated to the individual at the time consent is given.

Privacy Law permits consent to be given in different forms. Depending upon the level of sensitivity of the personal information, consent may not be required in writing. Consent may be obtained orally, or it may be given implicitly depending upon the nature of the personal information in question. Certainly, employers must be conscious of difficulties that they will face in establishing that consent was properly given without a written authorization.

An important exception to the general consent requirement exists under both the Alberta PIPA and the B.C. PIPA. Specifically, employee personal information may be collected, used or disclosed without the consent of the affected employee. Instead, organizations are required to give clear notification to the employee of the employer's intended practices, including the purposes behind the collection of the information.

This exemption to the consent requirement has allowed organizations in Alberta and British Columbia to implement a Privacy Law compliance program without the often difficult task of obtaining consent from existing employees.

The "Openness Principle"

In accordance with the "Openness Principle", an organization is also required to provide information regarding the security measures it has taken to protect the personal information.

Individuals are entitled under Privacy Law to know who controls their personal information and how to gain access to it. Organizations must also inform individuals as to the type of personal information held, as well as copies of any documentation explaining the organization's policies relating to its use and disclosure of personal information. Finally, the organization must inform individuals of the personal information that is being made available to related organizations such as subsidiaries.

An organization may make information on its policies and practices available in a variety of ways. Privacy Law anticipates that the method chosen depends on the nature of its business and other considerations.

While there is some flexibility in providing access to the personal information held by an organization, there are some specific obligations under Privacy Law relating to access. For example, requests to access personal information must be addressed within a reasonable time and at minimal or no cost to the individual.

The information requested must also be in a generally understandable form. Where the information is inaccurate, the individual is entitled under Privacy Law to insist that it be deleted or corrected by the organization.

HEALTH INFORMATION PRESENTS PITFALLS

Perhaps no type of information subject to Privacy Law raises as many potential pitfalls for employers as personal health information. Employers are regularly provided with information regarding the medical condition of their employees, often to excuse an absence from work or to substantiate an entitlement to an income replacement scheme such as a short-term disability plan.

Employers must be cognizant that the Privacy Law restrictions against collecting personal information unnecessary for the stated purpose applies equally to health information. Written confirmation from an employee's physician to justify an absence, for example, can be obtained without the need to identify the underlying medical condition. To require more would be a collection without a proper purpose in violation of Privacy Law regardless of the employee's willingness to comply with such a request.

The improper collection of employee medical information also puts the employer at risk of possible unauthorized uses or even disclosures outside of the organization, raising the specter of a host of employment-based claims in addition to those based in Privacy Law.

COMPLYING WITH PRIVACY LAW

Privacy Law requires employers to take positive steps to ensure compliance with the applicable legislation, including the following:

Review of Present Practices

Employers must review their present practices regarding the collection, use and disclosure of personal information to ensure that the necessary consent has been obtained from the individual.

While certain personal information can be collected, used and disclosed to third parties by the employer with implied, rather than express consent, written consent forms will be needed in many instances, including where personal health information is involved.

Establish Access/Retention Procedures

Consistent with the legislation's "Openness" principle, employers are required to make available information regarding the policies and practices in respect of the management of personal information.

Employers must produce a written statement, available to the public, describing the employer's information practices, the process for individuals, including employees, to obtain access to their personal information held by the employer, as well as the complaint process available under Privacy Law.

Employees are entitled to review the information held by the employer, subject to some excluded information, and to challenge the accuracy of the information. To administer these requests, every employer is obligated to appoint a privacy officer responsible for ensuring compliance with Privacy Law.

Further, employers are obligated to return or destroy personal information once it is no longer needed. The management of this practice should be administered through an express set of retention procedures.

Privacy Violations

Privacy Law provides for two separate avenues to sanction employers found to be in violation by the relevant privacy commission. First, there is an explicit right to sue for damages for breach of privacy available to any person whose privacy rights have been offended. The claim can be brought in provincial or federal court, depending upon which Act has been violated.

Second, the relevant privacy commissioner may proceed with a prosecution of an employer, as well as any officers, directors or employees who are found to have intentionally violated the applicable Privacy Law. Penalties in the range of $100,000 for employers and $10,000 for individuals can be assessed.[3]

---

[3]   The quantum of fines available differs under the various federal and provincial Privacy Laws.

Index

reinstatement obligations, 44–45
return to work obligations, 43
threats re unionization, 92
unfair labour practices, 92–93

**EMPLOYMENT
  APPLICATION FORMS,** 33

EMPLOYMENT CONTRACTS
confidentiality, 75
non-competition provision, 75–76
non-solicitation provision, 76
notice of termination, 74–75
patents and inventions, 76
purpose of employment, 75
remuneration, 76
termination provisions, 74–75
written contracts, 73–74

***EMPLOYMENT INSURANCE
  ACT***
amount of benefits, 38–39
application, 35
compassionate care benefits, 38
exclusions, 35
illness insurance premium
  reduction, 36–37
insurable earnings, 36
maternity benefits, 38
parental benefits, 38
premiums, 36
Record of Employment, 37
self-employed persons, 35
sickness benefits, 38
Social Insurance Numbers, 39–40
terminating employees, 37
work-sharing agreements, 37

***EMPLOYMENT PROTECTION
  FOR FOREIGN NATIONALS
  ACT (LIVE-IN CAREGIVERS
  AND OTHERS), 2009,*** 23

**EMPLOYMENT
  RELATIONSHIPS,** 1–2

EMPLOYMENT SECURITY, 84

***EMPLOYMENT STANDARDS
  ACT, 2000***
application, 1–2
complaints, 27–29
director liability, 29
discrimination in benefit plans
  prohibited, 26
equal pay for equal work, 25–26
hearings, 29
hours of work
• breaks, 6
• exemptions, 4–5
• managers and supervisors, 5
• overtime pay, 6–7
• requirements, 5–6
information postings, 30
investigations, 27–29
leave
• declared emergency leave, 17
• family medical leave, 16–17
• organ donor leave, 18
• parental leave, 13–15
• personal emergency leave, 15–16
• pregnancy leave, 13–15
• reservist leave, 18
lie detector tests, 26
overtime pay, 6–7
public holidays
• generally, 8–11
• retail businesses, 11–12
records, 3
sale of a business, 27
• building service providers,
  business transfer, 27
special types of employment
• domestic workers, 23
• homeworkers, 23
• hospitality industry/seasonal
  employees, 23
• local cartage and highway
  transport, 24
• residential care workers, 24
• temporary help agencies, 24–25
termination of employment
• notice of termination, 17–20, 21
• recall rights, 20–21